ISLAM
the Challenge
to the Church

Patrick Sookhdeo Ph.D., D.D.

Published by
Isaac Publishing
The Old Rectory
River Street
Pewsey
Wiltshire
SN9 5DB
UK

Designed by Inspiration by Design

Printed and bound by Biddles Ltd, King's Lynn

ISBN 0-9547835-4-9

CONTENTS

Different translations of the Qur'an can vary slightly in the numbering of the verses. If using another translation it may be necessary to look in the verses preceding or following the reference to find the same text. All quotations from the Qur'an in this book have been taken from the widely distributed translation *Interpretation of the Meanings of the Noble Qur'an in the English Language: A Summarized Version of At-Tabari, Al-Qurtabi and Ibn Kathir with comments from Sahih Al-Bukhari Summarized in One Volume*, by Muhammad Taqi-ud-Din Al Hilali and Muhammad Muhsin Khan, 15th revised edition (Riyadh: Darussalam, 1996).

A PERSONAL NOTE FROM
THE AUTHOR

I was born in Guyana, South America in 1947 and lived there until I was 12. Guyana in the 1950s was – and still is – very mixed in terms of ethnicity, culture and religion. There were Muslims, Hindus and Christians, and people of African, Asian and European descent as well as indigenous Amerindians.

But we all lived together in peace and harmony. We ate each other's food and celebrated each other's festivals. No faith sought to gain religious or political dominance. No faith felt threatened or intimidated by another one. No faith was legally advantaged or disadvantaged more than the others. I was brought up in a Muslim family and sent to *madrassa* [Qur'an school] at the age of $4^1/_2$. The imam did not teach us to hate or despise other faiths, or that it was our duty to attack other faiths; he simply taught us to chant the Qur'an.

Now I am a Christian and live in another multiethnic, multicultural, multifaith society, the UK. I remember in the 1960s how we immigrants did our best to assimilate into the majority culture and to become as British as we could as fast as we could. But nowadays some minorities have a different attitude. I am both grieved and alarmed to see how equality, peace and harmony in British society are fast disappearing, for which the main cause seems to be the egregious behaviour of a radical minority within one particular faith, Islam. There is such fear of radical

Islam that few voices dare to point out what is happening.

It does not have to be like this. I **know** that from my personal experience. Hundreds of thousands of other Guyanese of my age will have similar memories. The same inter-religious harmony has also existed in other places at other times. It **is** possible for faiths to live together in peace without one subjugating the rest.

The Iranian liberal Muslim writer, Amir Taheri, has pointed out how extraordinarily politicised Islam in the West has become, to the point where God is hardly mentioned in sermons. He says that the UK's 2,000 or so mosques are basically "a cover for a political movement", i.e. that British Islam has become "a political movement masquerading as a religion". Taheri suggests three reasons for this. Firstly, Muslims in the West come from a wide variety of backgrounds but are unable to continue here their historic sectarian feuds. So they lay aside theological issues and unite on other issues such as hatred of gay marriages or of Israel. Secondly, Western freedoms have allowed Islamic political movements to flourish, movements which are suppressed or banned in many parts of the Muslim world. Thirdly, there has been a rapprochement between British Islam and the extreme Left, which work together on issues such as anti-war, anti-America and anti-Israel.[1]

We need to guard our liberties, not take them for granted. Although we know that the gates of hell will not ultimately prevail against the Church which the Lord is building, there are sections of his Church which have disappeared completely in the face of the challenge of Islam, for example, North Africa which was once a major

---

1   Amir Taheri, "We don't do God, we do Palestine and Iraq" in *The Sunday Times* (12 February 2006)

centre of Christianity. Christians in Victoria State, Australia, are bitterly regretting that they did not oppose the passing of the Racial and Religious Tolerance Act in 2001 which now stifles their preaching and teaching. "We did not give enough thought to it at the time," some said to me in January 2006.

Another main challenge which Islam presents to the Church is the care of converts. Becoming a Christian was a difficult experience for me, with all its attendant trials and alienation. Being a Christian from a non-Western background is also very difficult, as I have lived through the end of colonialism and have also faced considerable racism from the white Christian community.

It is my hope and prayer that this book will help Christians in the West to think about the issues which surround Islam, so that they will be enabled to respond to the challenge of Islam before it is too late.

Patrick Sookhdeo
Pewsey, 18th February 2006

PREFACE

Islam is a religion of law, rituals and duties. A Muslim's worldview and values are derived from these essential Islamic principles, in just the same way that a Christian's worldview and values are derived from Christian spirituality.

The aim of this book is to help Christians in the West to understand Islam and the challenge which the rise of Islam in the West poses to the Church. While these challenges affect Christian individuals not only as Christians but also as members of society, this book will mainly focus on the challenge of Islam to the Church.[2]

The book is written from within a Western context of massive loss of confidence among Christians, accompanied by confusion, uncertainty and sometimes even shame. This context is the result of a process which became evident after the end of the Second World War, a process in which individualism, utilitarianism, materialism and hedonism gradually gained prominence and influence. Meanwhile duty, loyalty and even Christianity itself became increasingly scorned. The vacuum left by the virtual demise of Christianity was first filled by secular humanism but latterly Islam is gaining many converts from those with a spiritual hunger who are seeking a faith to follow. The more radical sections of Islam are in turn joining forces with traditionally

---

2   For more information on the societal challenge which Islam poses in the West, see *Islam in Britain: The British Muslim Community in February 2005* A report by the Institute for the Study of Islam and Christianity (Pewsey: Isaac Publishing, 2005).

atheistic movements such as the hard Left who share their anti-globalism, anti-capitalism sentiments and their deep-seated animosity towards Western liberal democracies. A third ally for the Islamism-Extreme Left partnership is found in liberal Christianity.

At the same time there has been an increasing sense of shame amongst some white Westerners, particularly Britons, who have been taught to believe the very worst about the British Empire. They feel they can do no right, and believe that because of the "sins" of earlier generations (such as colonialism and the Crusades) they have forfeited the right even to comment on other people's culture or religion. Thus, in preparation for the bicentenary of the abolition of the slave trade by the British Parliament, the Church of England, under the guidance of the Archbishop of Canterbury, made a statement apologising to the descendants of the slave trade's victims, but making no mention at all of the victory of abolition. This all-pervading shame and sense of ineligibility to critique non-Westerners may be one reason why (until recently) very few white Britons offered any criticism of the radical and violent aspects of Islam.

The accusation of Islamophobia is often levelled against those who draw attention to aspects of Islam which do not meet modern standards of human rights etc. It is important to recognise the distinction between Islam the religious ideology and Muslims the people who follow it. While it is possible and in some situations necessary to draw attention to negative aspects of a religious ideology, the attitude of Christians to Muslims as fellow human beings should always be one of love, compassion and concern.

It is important also to recognise that all faiths, including Christianity, have been misused by their followers at various times and places. We must acknowledge that atrocities and injustices have been perpetrated in the name of Christ, and we must avoid the pitfall of comparing the beautiful ideals of one faith with the less than perfect practices of another.

Although Islam is basically totalitarian in nature and dissent is rarely allowed, paradoxically there is and always has been a wide diversity of opinion within Islam, and numerous mutually intolerant divisions, sects and movements exist. Despite this there is a core orthodoxy which is fairly easy to identify and it is this "standard" Islam which will be our main focus. We will also look briefly at the differences between some of the major groupings and trends within Islam.

Islam is multi-faceted in a way that is unlike any other religion. In Islam there is no separation between sacred and secular, or between spiritual and material. Islam encompasses the social, legal, cultural, political and even military aspects of life. Because of this there is a serious problem of understanding with regard to Christians approaching Islam; many of the terms used by the two faiths are identical, giving the impression of a close similarity of thought-processes, and yet the meanings can be radically different.

Christians seeking to enter into dialogue with Muslims need to understand this core orthodoxy and inherent unity within the Islamic faith. Recent years have seen a rise in the phenomenological approach to other religions, which looks for commonalities between different faiths such as holy men, holy places or holy things. This approach does not suit Islam. Focusing on aspects of religious phenomena in Islam which are apparently held in common with Christianity does not lead to a correct understanding of Islam. This book will therefore attempt to look at Islam as a Muslim does, i.e. seeing the whole rather than the separate parts. While examining in turn a multiplicity of issues, each must always be understood in the light of the whole system that is Islam.

INTRODUCTION

The tragic events of September 11th 2001 spawned a huge interest in Islam, which has become a frequent topic of debate and analysis in Western media, society and Church. Added to this are factors such as the growth of Muslim minorities in the West, the "war on terrorism" (which so far has been largely a war on Islamic terrorism), the American-led incursions into Afghanistan and Iraq, the reactions to these of the Muslim community worldwide, Iran's proposed nuclear programme, and the international Muslim reaction against publication of cartoons of Muhammad, the prophet of Islam. All these issues have brought Islam to centre stage and are forcing a radical re-think of Western opinion on the nature of Islam.

Formerly driven chiefly by factors such as post-colonial guilt and sympathy for the perceived underdog, the debate is now fuelled by fresh theories such as a revisionist approach to history, by Samuel Huntington's thesis of an inevitable "clash of civilisations" (between Islam and the West), and by a philosophical and linguistic deconstructionism that negates all absolutes.

Interestingly there has also been a dramatic change in Muslim presentations of their faith to outsiders. This phenomenon began before September 11th 2001, but the rate has increased dramatically since that date. The impetus is the desire to defend Islam from any negative criticism and to present it as entirely positive and devoid of anything blameworthy throughout its history. This has been described as "the turbanning of the mind". Islam appears to aspire literally to rewrite the text books.

Amidst these urgently competing voices, it is small wonder that the Christian Church is in a state of confusion as to the attitude she should adopt towards this other major world faith, seemingly sharing so much doctrine in common with Christianity and yet so very different in manifestation. We shall first look at the nature of Islam, and compare it with Christianity. Key contemporary issues will be examined in turn, each one being crucial to the way in which Islam is manifested in contemporary society. Finally, we look at some of the practical issues of Christian-Muslim relations in the West.

Contemporary Islam increasingly focuses on classical Islam and its manifestations. Classical Islam was formulated in the first few centuries after Muhammad, and in the tenth century AD it was agreed that the work had been completed. The consensus (in Sunni Islam, which comprises at least 80% of Muslims today) is that no alteration can now be made to the regulations laid down by the early Islamic scholars. The process by which such change could be made is known as *ijtihad* and this is what both liberal Muslims and Islamists claim to be doing as they seek to reform Islam in their respective directions. However, among the great mass of Muslims in general there is enormous fear of making any alterations to the traditional rulings, as this would be deemed blasphemy or apostasy.

Thus it is effectively impossible to change or adapt Islam. Consequently there is an inevitable conflict between certain aspects of Islam and some modern societal norms. This conflict is far more than just a question of mental anguish for the individual, because a vital part of Islam is living out one's faith in society.

Faith, to a Muslim, is not merely personal but has social, political and cultural implications. A typical Muslim believes that their faith must impact the society in which they live and must contribute to the Islamic character of that society. This political aspect appears to have become the predominant feature of Islam in the West. It is only the relatively few liberal Muslims who would consider flouting orthodoxy by trying to adapt their faith to integrate into modern society.

The late Dr Zaki Badawi, who was president of the Muslim College in London, expressed the underlying assumption within Islam that Muslims must live in an Islamic society, ordered according to the teachings of Islam.

> The history of Islam as a faith is also the history of a state and a community of believers living by Divine law. The Muslims, jurists and theologians have always expounded Islam as both a Government and a faith. This reflects the historical fact that Muslims, from the start, lived under their own law. Muslim theologians naturally produced a theology with this in view – it is a theology of the majority. Being a minority was not seriously considered or even contemplated.[3]

Badawi went on to explain that there is no consensus within Islam about how Muslims should live as a minority within a non-Muslim majority. Thus Islam is bound to impact the societies in which it finds itself. This impact is felt in six primary areas, as defined by Rev. Albrecht Hauser: spiritual, theological, missiological, societal, political and in the area of justice.

> Islam is a spiritual movement, which throughout history has had a strangling effect on the Christian Church. There has been much oppression and suffering, since Islam considers Christians to have gone astray and since Islam rejects and considers the central beliefs of Christians to be obsolete.

---

3   Zaki Badawi, *Islam in Britain* (London: Taha Publishers, 1981) p.26

Theologically the whole concept of incarnation, the vicarious death of Christ and his redemptive cross is rejected in Islam, so also is the Trinitarian understanding of God. The cross is veiled and the challenge for the Christian Church is to understand and happily confess why Jesus is truly God and truly man. Since Islam believes in the unity of the sacred and secular, and of the state and religion, it also poses a political challenge. Islam needs to be viewed in many ways as an ideology seeking to gain political power. Islam is not only a religion in the Western sense, but also an ideology with a total claim on the society and political life of its adherents, ruled by divine, rather than secular law. Since the divine law (*shari'a*) is considered superior to all man-made laws of secular societies there is always a tendency to push for other legislation to be made to conform to the *shari'a*.[4]

Western Christians who are concerned to react in an appropriate, loving, scriptural and Christ-like way to the presence of Islam in their societies must have a clear understanding of the nature of Islam – its theology, ethics and culture – so as to discern where there is common ground and where there are differences. This will help in the crucial decisions that have to be made on how to approach Muslims, and how to respond to the approaches that they make to Christians.

---

4   Albrecht Hauser, unpublished lecture, 23 January 2006

1

UNDERSTANDING ISLAM

Basic theology

Definition of Islam
The term "Islam" is defined as follows: "The Arabic word 'Islam' simply means 'submission'... In a religious context it means complete submission to the will of God."[5] Muslims sometimes claim that Islam means peace, or is derived from the same root as the Arabic word for peace. However, this is not true linguistically. *"Salam"* [peace] and "Islam" may sound similar but they are unrelated and do not come from the same root.

Muhammad's life
Muslims believe that Muhammad was the final prophet, after whom no other prophets will come. All previous prophets were only relevant for their time.

According to Islamic teaching, Muhammad (c. 570 – 632 AD) was an Arabian merchant who at the age of 40 began to receive a series of messages for mankind, which Muslims believe came from the angel Gabriel. (Christians will of course question whether the angel who announced the birth of Christ could 600 years later have brought a message so contrary to the teachings of Christ.) He and his early followers were mocked and

---

5   *Understanding Islam and the Muslims* (The Islamic Affairs Department, The Embassy of Saudi Arabia, Washington DC, 1989)

persecuted in his home town of Mecca so they began to flee to Medina, with Muhammad himself finally joining them in 622. In Medina Muhammad set up an Islamic state, with himself as judge, ruler and military commander.[6]

The attitude of most Muslims to Muhammad is best described as veneration. This is a paradoxical aspect of Islam, a faith which in theory affirms the believer's direct access to God without the need for any intercessor. Accordingly, Muhammad **should** be viewed by Muslims as simply a human channel for God's revelation. In practice, however, Muhammad's figure towers over Islam not just as its founder, but as the "perfect man" who was divinely inspired not only in his Qur'anic revelations, but in all his sayings and deeds, thus making his life normative for all times. "As a messenger he is the last and greatest, about whom the early messengers have predicted and who thus completes the process of revelation. He is therefore the Perfect Ideal for Mankind, the perfect servant of Allah and hence the most complete and ideally balanced manifestation of the attributes of Allah."[7] He is considered infallible, free from sin, and serves as the supreme example whom all Muslims are obliged to emulate in every small detail.

Muhammad is also seen as the intercessor with God who can change the divine decrees and admit those he intercedes for into paradise. Love for Muhammad (and his family) is strongly instilled into most Muslim children. Many Muslims, especially in the Indian subcontinent, hold that Muhammad was created from an eternal heavenly substance (Muhammadan light) that pre-existed with God. He is a logos-like figure similar to Christ – a sinless mediator and intercessor.

---

6   All the sources on Muhammad's life are Muslim and none of them was written earlier than 150 years after his death.

7   *Islam: The Essentials* (Markfield, UK: The Islamic Foundation, 1974)

A main concern of Muslims is the person of Muhammad who must be protected from any criticism or slight. Protecting his honour is an obligation on all. Any suspected denigration of Muhammad immediately creates disturbances and riots in many Muslim countries and communities, more so than blasphemy against Allah himself.

Scriptures

> The Qur'an is a record of the exact words revealed by God through the Angel Gabriel to the Prophet Muhammad. It was memorized by Muhammad and then dictated to his Companions, and written down by scribes, who crosschecked it during his lifetime. Not one word of its 114 chapters, *suras*, has been changed over the centuries, so that the Qur'an is in every detail the unique and miraculous text which was revealed to Muhammad fourteen centuries ago.[8]

The original is believed by Muslims to be inscribed in Arabic on a tablet in heaven, hence the great reverence accorded to it and to the Arabic language. Islam has a similar concept of revelation to Mormonism.

However, non-Muslim scholars and early Islamic writings have a different understanding of how the Qur'an developed. Early Islamic sources say that it was not written down until after Muhammad's death. It is also clear that there were many versions of the Qur'an in existence for some time, until Caliph Uthman ordered the suppression of all but one version between 650 and 656. However, despite Uthman's efforts (and contrary to what Muslims believe), two versions of the Qur'an remained as late as the mid-twentieth century, the minority version being used by some North African Muslims.

Non-Muslim scholars have also shown how many of the teachings of the Qur'an resemble a distorted version

---

8   *Understanding Islam and the Muslims* (The Islamic Affairs Department, The Embassy of Saudi Arabia, Washington DC, 1989)

of Christianity and Judaism. Indeed it is not necessary to be much of a scholar to see this. Muhammad would not have required an angelic messenger to provide him with the Qur'an; he could have composed it on the basis of what he learnt from Arab Christians he met, perhaps seeking to correct and purify a faith which he could see the Christians themselves had rather a poor grasp of.

Second in importance to the Qur'an are a collection of traditions about what Muhammad and his earliest followers said and did, known as the *hadith*. The *hadith* are used by Islamic scholars to interpret the Qur'an (which in many places is vague and ambiguous), i.e. to indicate how the Qur'an should be understood and therefore what Muslims should do in any particular situation. The example of Muhammad and the first Muslims provides guidance on areas where the Qur'an is silent or incomprehensible.

Allah (the Arabic term for "God")
The three most important characteristics of God in Islam are his oneness (*tawhid*), his transcendent otherness and his power. "*Allahu Akbar*", the traditional Muslim cry, means "God is great". It is a terrible blasphemy and unforgivable sin to associate anything with God; hence the vehement rejection of the Christian concept of the Trinity and of the phrase "Son of God".

There is much debate currently amongst Christians about the etymology of the word "Allah" and several theories are in circulation. It certainly existed in the Arabic language in pre-Islamic times, carrying the meaning of the supreme God, creator of the universe. But trying to track down the meaning a word had many centuries ago is not really very illuminating; after all the English word "God" is derived from a pagan term used in pre-Christian times, but rightly this does not trouble English-speaking Christians who give it their own meaning based on the Bible. Languages do evolve over time and words are "borrowed" from one context to be used in another. What is important today is to grasp what Muslims mean when they use the word "Allah". (See page 50.)

"Allah" is the word in both ancient and modern Arabic for "God". It is used by Arab Christians to mean their heavenly Father. It is found in the Arabic Bible wherever the word "God" is needed, for example, Genesis 1, John 1:1 and John 3:16. It was also used by Arab Christians in pre-Islamic times.

Eschatology
Muslims believe there will be catastrophic signs of the End Times which include the rise of the *dajjal* (antichrist) and the return of Jesus as a Muslim to defeat the *dajjal* and convert everyone to Islam. Most Muslims, and especially Shi'as, also believe in a coming End-Time messianic figure, the Mahdi, who will rule justly for a period. This will be followed by a general resurrection on the final Day of Judgement in which humans will be judged according to their deeds. The wicked (including all non-Muslims) will be assigned to hell, the just will enter paradise. Both paradise and hell are subdivided into various levels. Jesus is in only the second level of paradise, Moses is far above him in the sixth and Abraham in the seventh. Muhammad is in the highest level of paradise, just below God's throne. Some good Muslims – and especially those who die as martyrs for the cause of Islam – may go straight to paradise but many Muslims will have to spend time suffering in a purgatory-like stage before being allowed into paradise.

Angels and jinn
Angels are God's supernatural messengers created from light who watch over humans and record their good and bad deeds. The greatest angel is Gabriel [Jibrail] who is also called the Holy Spirit [*Ruh ul'Amin*]. Jinn are spirits created by God from fire. Although some *jinn* are good, many of them are evil. Satan is sometimes described as a *jinn*, sometimes as an angel.

The five pillars
These five basic requirements of Islam mark Muslims as distinct from followers of other religions, signifying their submission, obedience, dependence and willingness to sacrifice.

1. Frequent recitation of the basic creedal declaration of faith [*shahada* or *kalima*]: "There is no god but God, and Muhammad is the apostle⁹ of God." It is significant that Muhammad is included in this declaration – submission to God signifies submission to Muhammad's message and example.

2. Ritual prayers [*salat*] in the Arabic language at five appointed daily hours (dawn, noon, mid-afternoon, sunset and nightfall), accompanied by ceremonial washings and postures.

3. Fasting [*sawm*] from sunrise to sunset during the month of Ramadan. The fast includes abstinence from food, drink, sexual relations and smoking. Nowadays there is a huge celebratory feast every evening, as a result of which more food is consumed in Muslim countries during Ramadan than in a normal month.

4. The compulsory giving of alms [*zakat*] as a proportion of one's wealth (usually 2.5% for Sunnis).

---

9   The Arabic term *rasul* can be translated apostle, prophet or messenger.

Some goes to help the poor and some to help those who fight in *jihad*.[10] Most Muslims hold that *zakat* cannot normally be given to non-Muslims. The definition given in the glossary of *The Noble Qur'an*, a widely distributed English translation of the Qur'an, states clearly that *zakat* is "for the benefit of the poor in the Muslim community".[11]

5. The pilgrimage to Mecca [*hajj*] is compulsory at least once in a lifetime for those in good health who can afford it. This includes wearing special clothes and engaging in specified rites, including circling seven times the *ka'ba* (the cube-like building at the centre of the Great Mosque).

Jihad

While not normally included in the five pillars (though some Muslims do add it as a sixth pillar), the struggle for Islam [*jihad*] is one of the most basic religious duties glorified in the Qur'an and *hadith* and prescribed in Islamic law [*shari'a*]. "In all such cases, Jihad is as much a primary duty of the Muslims concerned as are the daily prayers or fasting".[12]

There are non-violent aspects of *jihad* such as financial sacrifice, the spiritual battle for moral purity, and using the tongue and hands to correct what is wrong and support what is right, but "in the language of Shari'ah this word is used particularly for a war that is waged solely in the name of Allah against those who practise oppression as enemies of Islam".[13]

---

10   Laleh Bakhtiar, *Encyclopedia of Islamic Law: A Compendium of Major Schools* (Chicago, ABC International Group, 1996) p.241

11   Muhammad Taqi-ud-Din Al-Hilali and Muhammad Muhsin Khan, *Interpretation of the Meanings of the Noble Qur'an in the English Language: A Summarized Version of At-Tabari, Al-Qurtabi and Ibn Kathir with comments from Sahih Al-Bukhari Summarized in One Volume* 15th revised edition (Riyadh: Darussalam, 1996) p.824

12   Abul A'la Mawdudi, *Towards Understanding Islam* (Birmingham: U.K.I.M. Dawah Centre, 1980) p.73

13   Abul A'la Mawdudi, *Towards Understanding Islam* p.73

The Noble Qur'an defines *jihad* in its glossary as follows:

> Holy fighting in the Cause of Allah or any other kind of effort to make Allah's Word (i.e. Islam) superior. *Jihad* is regarded as one of the fundamentals of Islam.[14]

A footnote to sura 2, verse 190 (a key verse on jihad) states: *"Al-jihad* (holy fighting) in Allah's Cause (with full force of numbers and weaponry) is given the utmost importance in Islam and is one of its pillars (on which it stands)." It goes on to explain that *jihad* is the means by which Islam and its creed are established and propagated. According to this footnote, *jihad* is an obligatory duty for every Muslim and any who try to avoid it or even in their hearts to not wish to fulfil it "dies with one of the qualities of a hypocrite".[15] Those who raise armed *jihad* to the status of a "sixth pillar" make it a required duty for Muslims.

In early Islam *jihad* was seen as the God-given method for the expansion of Islam's political domain until all polytheists convert (or are killed) and Jews and Christians humbly submit themselves to Islamic domination. This understanding was consolidated in the teachings of classical Islam formulated over the next few centuries.[16]

Territory

Linked to the interpretation of *jihad* as the means of expanding Islam's political control is the classical Islamic concept of dividing the world into two domains: the house of Islam (*Dar al-Islam*) where political power is in the hands of Muslims and *shari'a* is enforced, and the house of war (*Dar al-harb*). It is a religious duty for

---

14   *Interpretation of the meanings of The Noble Qur'an in the English language* (translated by Al-Hilali and Khan) p.809
15   As above p.47
16   For details of this and the Islamic sources, see the author's *Understanding Islamic Terrorism* (Pewsey: Isaac Publishing, 2004)

Muslims until the Day of Judgement to fight the house of war and transform it into the house of Islam.

Religious territoriality is an essential part of Islam, and Muslims are very conscious of whether or not they "control" any particular piece of land. They believe they must never yield any of their territory to non-Muslims, which is one of the reasons that many Muslims cannot conceive of any resolution to the Palestinian issue apart from the establishment of an Islamic state in place of Israel (a state in which Jews may or may not be permitted to live as a minority). The concept also has implications in the West, both in terms of town planning and in terms of how church leaders might choose to respond to requests by local Muslims for using church premises for their activities. Once a place has been used for Islamic worship, it is considered to "belong" to Islam for ever. (See also pages 69-70, 77-78.)

Shari'a

Islamic law, [*shari'a*] is based on Qur'an and *hadith*, and is an all-encompassing legalistic structure for the Islamic way of life, determining what is forbidden [*haram*] and what is permitted [*halal*]. It contains detailed instructions for personal daily life and how to practise the pillars of Islam. The spectrum is subdivided into various degrees of obligatory, recommended, neutral, objectionable and forbidden. There is no individuality and no choice. In the eyes of most Muslims there is also no potential for any change to the *shari'a* regulations formulated in the eighth and ninth centuries AD.

Shari'a covers personal devotional life, family life, criminal law, the conduct of war, international relations and every aspect of life. *Shari'a* is given by Allah, the only sovereign legislator, for all times, and its implementation is an absolute command. It is also the only criterion of right and wrong:

> The Shari'ah itself is therefore the ultimate criterion of
> justice and mercy, and cannot and ought not to be
> measured against human standards.[17]

This statement becomes very relevant when it is considered how far the *shari'a* does deviate from modern standards of human rights and religious liberty. It is discriminatory against women and against non-Muslims. For example, the compensation payable to an individual after an injury is less for a woman and for a non-Muslim than for a Muslim man with the same injury. Likewise the value of their testimony in a law-court is less than that of a Muslim man. There is a whole raft of legislation in the *shari'a* to restrict the rights of non-Muslims (see pages 66-68).

Da'wa [Islamic mission]
Islam is a missionary religion and all Muslims have a duty to witness to their faith and win converts.

> The Qur'an clearly states that witnessing to the Truth in a
> manner that would leave mankind with no justifiable
> ground to deny it is the only purpose behind constituting
> you as a distinct Ummah (community), named Muslims ...
> this is no ordinary duty: it is a duty enjoined on you by
> Allah. It is a Divine command and a Divine call.[18]

Islamic *da'wa*, however, goes beyond gaining individual converts. It is seen as a communal responsibility aimed at extending the political and legal domain of Islam at the expense of all "unbelievers" [*kuffar*]. It includes the strategy of keeping non-Muslim society – including the press and legislature – occupied with Islamic agendas, as part of the process of making society conform to Islam.

---

17   Khurram Murad, *Shariah: The Way of Justice* (Leicester, The Islamic Foundation 1981) p.6
18   Abul A'la Mawdudi, *Witnesses Unto Mankind* translated by Khurram Murad (Birmingham, U.K.I.M, 1986) pp. 2-3

Islam replaces Christianity
Muslims hold that the Qur'an replaced the Old and New Testaments as God's written revelation valid today for all human beings. They claim that the text of the Bible has been corrupted by Jews and Christians, so is untrustworthy. At the same time Muhammad replaces Jesus as the Perfect Man, the God-given perfect example. The Qur'an even asserts that Jesus himself predicted the coming of Islam and Muhammad.[19]

While asserting that Muhammad is a normal human being with no supernatural powers who served simply as God's mouthpiece, Muslims have in practice elevated him into a Christ-like figure (see page 14). So, while paying lip service to their belief in Jewish and Christian scriptures and prophets, Muslims actually claim that Islam has superseded them and is the only valid religion for humanity today. It could be termed the ultimate "replacement theology".

Social issues

No separation of religion and state/society
Most Muslims consider the secular division of religion from the state as rebellion against God. They firmly believe in the unity of state and religion – Islam is both religion and state. Mosques, in contrast to churches, have always been centres of political agitation and intrigue. This view is the reason for the constant demands for state recognition of separate self-governing Muslim communities in the West. It also fuels the demands within Muslim-majority countries for the creation of true Islamic states governed by *shari'a*. In many Muslim countries, the state is intimately involved in religious affairs, often controlling the mosques and the clerical establishment as well as

---

19   Sura 61, verse 6

Islamic charitable foundations. Opposition to regimes is often expressed in Islamic terms, thus gaining respectability and popular support.

Individual and community
Central to a proper understanding of Islam is the realisation that the community takes priority over the individual. Thus an individual's needs and choices must always be subjected to the good of the wider group in any case of conflict of interest. This wider group would be firstly the (extended) family, and secondly the entire Muslim community worldwide, the *umma*.

The *umma* is a global community of faith, which is meant to transcend race, nationality and culture. It is this that gives the Muslim his or her primary identity. This is not just a theoretical concept but is meant to have practical application in that when one Muslim is suffering or ill-treated the whole Muslim community should rally to his or her defence. The result is that Muslims tend to forget their differences and "close ranks" in the face of an outside threat. Muslims also show a passionate and unwavering loyalty to each other when it comes to advancing the cause of Islam or defending its honour.

The same principle of community taking priority over the individual is reflected in the coercive nature of the *shari'a*.

Loyalties
For many Muslims, loyalty to the global Muslim community (the *umma*) overrides loyalty to any nation-state. In the orthodox view, politics is the means of advancing the cause of the whole worldwide Muslim community, of expanding Muslim control over as much territory as possible and governing it according to the *shari'a*. According to this view, Muslims in non-Muslim states

have an overriding loyalty to further the cause of Islamising their host-societies even when this undermines their loyalty to the state.

Because of the differences, disunity and fragmentation which exist in the Islamic world, there has arisen a desire to create unity by re-establishing the Islamic caliphate which came to an end in 1924 when Mustafa Kemal Atatürk abolished the Ottoman caliphate and proclaimed the Republic of Turkey.

The issue of loyalties is a point of contention within contemporary Islam, as the classical position described above comes into conflict with the concept of belonging to a nation-state, a concept to which some modern Muslims do subscribe but which many others believe is un-Islamic.

Spirituality,[20] morality and culture

Focus on the external

Islam is often seen primarily as a religion of externals, in which outward conformity to rituals and rules is often considered more important than the question of inner sincerity. It is thus a religion which lends itself to enforcement by the state. For example, some Muslims believe that the recitation of the creed, even without inner conviction, is sufficient to convert a person to Islam. Another example is the Muslim concept of fasting, which is very much a communal and visible act, which must be seen to be done. This is in complete contrast to Jesus' instructions on fasting in which he specifically told his followers to try not to let other people realise that they were fasting (Matthew 6:16-18). Christian fasting is a private

---

20   There are a number of useful works on Islamic spirituality to which the reader is referred
      for a more detailed survey than is possible here. For example Constance E. Padwick
      Muslim Devotions: a Study of Prayer-Manuals in Common Use (London: SPCK, 1961);
      Seyyed Hossein Nasr *Islamic Art and Spirituality* (Ipswich: Golgonoosa Press, 1987);
      Thomas McElwain, a convert to Islam also called Ali Hayder *Spirituality: Christian and
      Islamic Parallels* (London: BookExtra, 2001).

act of self-denial between the individual and God. Muslim fasting is a public act which, hard though it may be through the hours of daylight, involves a daily banquet of vast quantities of delicacies.

The whole issue of the relationship of faith to Islam and of the term "Muslim" to the term "believer" as well as the need or otherwise for inner belief has historically been a subject of much debate within Islam. The Sufi movement within Islam (see page 42) emphasises the inner life and personal devotion to God. Muslims may also seek an inner spiritual experience through Muhammad veneration (widely practised on the Indian subcontinent) and various non-orthodox practices such as the ecstatic ceremonies of the whirling dervishes, the self-injury of many Shi'a sects and visiting the shrines of Muslim saints.

Given the emphasis on externals, it is perhaps little surprise that Islam primarily concentrates on material blessings rather than, say, the delights of fellowship with God. Paradise is full of sensual pleasures in which there are beautiful women, couches covered with brocades, plentiful wine and luscious fruits. Essentially it is the place where that which is forbidden on earth becomes allowed. There are today some Muslims who are seeking to interpret these heavenly promises in spiritual terms. They look forward to seeing at last in paradise the "unseeable" Allah, even if only for a moment. But historically the understanding has been literal and physical and still is for many Muslims today.

Fear and lack of assurance of salvation
The Muslim's submission to God is borne out of a fear of his sovereignty and overwhelming power. There are a variety of beliefs among Muslims about getting to paradise, but the bottom line is that God is remote and does as he wills in all things, so the outcome of God's

judgement is unpredictable: he will save or condemn as he pleases and will not necessarily take into account the individual's conduct while on earth. Therefore, in spite of obedience to *shari'a*, living a pious life and performing good works, few can be sure of their eternal destiny. Even those who believe that all Muslims will eventually get to paradise, hold that some may have to undergo a period of frightful punishment first. The only sure way to go straight to paradise – avoiding any punishment on the way – is to die as a martyr in *jihad*.

Freedom of conscience

Muslims have no freedom or choice in matters of religion. Islam is a one-way street which once entered cannot be forsaken. Leaving Islam is seen as treachery against Allah and against society, and therefore the penalty is death, as laid down in the *shari'a*. In addition there are a host of other legal penalties for apostates from Islam.

Some modern states enforce the death penalty, but even where this is not enshrined in the law of the land converts from Islam may find themselves punished by the authorities on some other pretext or intimidated and victimised by family and community who feel shamed by the "traitor". Many are physically attacked and some are even murdered.

Vulnerability and superiority

Richard Chartres, the Bishop of London, has said, "There is an immense sense in Islam of the superiority of Islam to everything else."[21] Believing that it is the final and ultimate religion, Islam finds it difficult to affirm other faiths. One symptom of this is the fact that all of history prior to Muhammad is termed "the age of

---

21   Quoted by Andrew Carey in "Islam's confused identity" in *The Church of England Newspaper* (August 28, 2003)

ignorance" implying that nothing good can be learnt from it. Neither can anything good be learnt from later non-Islamic contexts. Muslims will very rarely accept blame for evils committed in the name of Islam, or apologise to their victims. The shame of losing face would keep many from even contemplating such an admission.

Muslims usually interpret confession of guilt by others as a sign of despicable weakness. Likewise, humility and forgiveness are not seen as virtues but as weaknesses. They hold that the appropriate reaction to being wronged is to seek revenge. Muslims have very long historical memories and continue to remember with outrage the defeats and humiliations of many centuries ago even if they were suffered by far distant parts of the *umma*. What Charles Moore has termed "pre-emptive self-abasement"[22] – the Western (and perhaps especially British) penchant for offering profuse apologies for all faults, past and present, real or imagined – is at best useless, but more likely to be counter-productive. This is important for Christians to remember when engaged in "dialogue" or debate with Muslims.

Power and honour
An important part of Islamic self-understanding is the concept that power and honour rightly belong to Muslims. The basis of this is found in the Qur'an (sura 63, verse 8)

> ... But honour, power and glory belong to Allah and to His Messenger (Muhammad), and to the believers"[23]

The Arabic word translated here as "honour, power and glory" appears in some other translations simply as

---

22   Charles Moore, "But, Archbishop, this is the bleak mid-winter for many Christians", in *The Daily Telegraph* (10 December 2005)

"honour". The longer translation correctly conveys the connotations of dominion and control which Muslims understand when they read this text. For Muslims temporal power, the advance of the Islamic faith, military victory and the prestige of Muslim people are all intrinsically linked to this promise. Humiliation and defeat are against God's plan for his people and when these occur they cause grave anguish to Muslims as they have no theology to deal with such situations.

> By abandoning Jihad (may Allah protect us from that) Islam is destroyed and the Muslims fall into an inferior position; their honour is lost, their lands are stolen, their rule and authority vanish.[24]

As Bishop Richard Chartres has said, Islam's sense of its own superiority

> is in terrible full-frontal collision with the evident inferiority of Muslim societies, technically, politically, economically, militarily. And the crisis in Islam (it's not so much a battle between East and West, Christians and Muslims, it's a battle in Islam) comes from the terrible collision of this sense of superiority with the evident inferiority in so many other ways which causes bewilderment and fierce debate on how we are going to get out of this bind.[25]

There is no real critical assessment within Islam of it own history and thus the glorification of early Islam and its expansion is seen as a Golden Age of Islam, which needs to be recreated in order finally to conquer the

---

23   Muhammad Taqi-ud-Din Al-Hilali and Muhammad Muhsin Khan *Interpretation of the Meanings of the Noble Qur'an in the English Language: A Summarized Version of At-Tabari, Al-Qurtabi and Ibn Kathir with comments from Sahih Al-Bukhari Summarized in One Volume* 15th revised edition (Riyadh: Darussalam, 1996). Different translations of the Qur'an can vary slightly in the numbering of the verses. If using another translation it may be necessary to look in the verses preceding or following this reference to find the same text. All quotations from the Qur'an in this book are taken from this widely distributed translation.

24   *Interpretation of the meanings of The Noble Qur'an in the English language* (translated by Al-Hilali and Khan) p.47

25   Quoted by Andrew Carey in "Islam's confused identity" in *The Church of England Newspaper* (August 28, 2003)

whole world for Islam.

Shame and guilt

Contrary to Christianity, it is shame rather than guilt which is the guiding principle in Islam. Shame is most easily defined by looking at its opposite, honour. Honour includes self-esteem and dignity, and the good opinion of others. It depends very much on the reputation of an individual and his family for generosity, morality, good behaviour, courage, good marriages, piety and loyalty to kin. The individual is expected to suppress his or her personal needs and interests if they interfere with family or community honour.

Public loss of face is the greatest possible shame, so blunt criticism (seen as a personal insult) must be avoided and praise must preface any indirect criticism, which must never be given in front of others.

Honour is more important than truth and even than life itself. Honour, of which a large part is the appearance of morality and the reputation for morality, is more important than morality itself. The deep fear of the loss of honour explains why some will kill people they love rather than be disgraced. If an incident causing loss of honour is not avenged, a man becomes permanently dishonoured and shamed. Sullied honour demands payment to restore the balance – payment ruled by traditional rituals of mediation and reconciliation. Ignoring these rituals leaves the offender open to violent revenge not only against himself but also against his family.

Women and family honour

A family's honour is especially bound up in the behaviour of its women who must be seen to dress and behave modestly. Maintaining proper relationships between the sexes is the responsibility of a man of honour who must control the women in his family so that they do nothing unseemly. Any hint of a sexual misdemeanour is considered a crime against family honour and must be punished to restore the depleted honour account.

Honour killings
The phrase "honour killings" generally refers to the practice of killing female family members who have behaved in an improper way. So strong is the drive to restore family honour that many women and girls have been killed for apparently minor offences, such as speaking to an unrelated man. They are often killed on the basis of a mere accusation, without proof of their crime. In societies where the concept of honour killing is very strong, for example Pakistan, the law enforcement agencies will do little or nothing to punish the murderer. It has recently become clear that many honour killings occur also within the Muslim communities of Western Europe.

The Muslim family
Muslim families tend to be conservative and patriarchal; the oldest male is usually recognised as head of the extended family, and fathers are the source of authority and discipline. The relationship between husband and wife is not expected to be close and fond; it is more a practical arrangement – one is the provider of money, the other the provider of sons. A man may have up to four wives if he treats them all equally. The closest family bond is often between a mother and her sons.

The extended family determines an individual's identity, position and status in society and to a large extent the chance of success and wealth. People are proud of their family connections and lineage. Loyalty to the family takes precedence over personal needs, obligations to friends or the demands of a job. A person's first allegiance will always be to their relatives, and a basic rule is that no one can really be trusted except family members. The family is the main source of emotional and economic security, and relatives are expected to help each other, including financial help when necessary.

The family is the most important factor in all decisions, including matters of religion, marriage and jobs. All social institutions are imagined as family: rulers see their citizens as their children and themselves as fathers of the nation. The same applies to teachers, employers, and political and religious leaders.

Women
In pre-Islamic Arabia women of the elite strata of society could be active participants, even leaders, in a wide range of community activities including warfare and religion. On the other hand poorer women were regarded as mere chattels of men, and female infanticide was practised. Such freedoms as the women had were curtailed when Islam was established, for its institution of patrilineal patriarchal marriage brought a social transformation. Muslims often claim that Muhammad improved the situation of women, but they usually fail to add that he also fixed their status for ever at a seventh century level.

The position accorded to women in the *shari'a* is certainly not one of equality with men. The various regulations concerned with women indicate an underlying, if unspoken, assumption that women are inferior to men in intelligence, morals and religion. They are therefore considered a source of temptation to men, and must be protected from their own weaknesses. This is tied up with the concept that a family's honour resides in its womenfolk. The primary requirement of a woman is obedience to her husband (rather than to God directly). Some Islamic scholars argue that most women will go to hell. Because of this aspect of Islam, it is rare for Muslim women and girls to be as well taught in their religion as the men and boys are. Most women therefore tend to follow folk Islam and may be very ignorant of the teachings of true Islam. Ironically, it is the women who watch over the faith of the family and ensure that the traditions of Islam are transmitted to the next generation, while the men are more prominent in public affairs.

Taqiyya [dissimulation, permitted deceit]
It often comes as a surprise to realise that protective deceit and dissimulation are an intrinsic part of Islam, permitted in certain specific situations, one of which is war, i.e. the defence of Islam. Some Muslims also hold that it is permissible to break agreements made with non-Muslims, believing such contracts to be valid only as long as they serve the cause of Islam. It is important for non-Muslims interacting with Muslims to be aware of the existence of *taqiyya*, as the concept of "defending Islam" can be interpreted very broadly and may lead to outright lying. What is said in English to Christians one day might be totally contradicted the next day by the same leaders speaking to Muslims, perhaps in Urdu or Arabic. For example, Hamid Ali, spiritual leader of a mosque in Beeston, West Yorkshire, UK called Al-Madina Masjid, publicly condemned the London bombings of 7th July 2005. But in a secretly taped conversation with a Bangladeshi-origin undercover reporter from *The Sunday Times* he said the 7/7 bombings were a "good" act and praised the bombers as "children" of firebrand cleric Abdullah al-Faisal who has made statements such as: "The only way forward is for you, the Muslims, to kill the *kufrs* [non-believers]." [26]

---

26   "British imam praises London Tube bombers" in *The Sunday Times* (12 February 2006)

As Dr Taj Hargey, Chairman of the Muslim Education Centre, Oxford explained on British television:

> We have one vocabulary in private and we have another vocabulary for the public domain and that's why you don't hear it because you're the public domain.[27]

Islam nominally places a high value on truth and one of the 99 names of Allah is *al-Haqq* [the Reality, the Supreme Truth]. Alongside this runs the doctrine of *taqiyya* which was first developed for dealing with situations of persecution where Muslims could save their lives by concealing their true beliefs. The Qur'anic basis is sura 16, verse 106, which absolves Muslims from Allah's wrath if they are forced into outward disbelief while in their hearts they remain true Muslims.

> Whoever disbelieved in Allah after his belief, except him who is forced thereto and whose heart is at rest with Faith; but such as open their breasts to unbelief, on them is wrath from Allah, and theirs will be a great torment.

Various *hadith* provide more details of when lying is permissible, typically in three situations: to one's wife, in war, and for the purpose of reconciliation. *Taqiyya* is particularly strong amongst Shi'a Muslims but also practised by Sunnis.

At a Palestine Solidarity Movement conference held at Georgetown University, Washington D.C. (17-19 February 2006) two workshops looked at how the participants could win Christians to their cause (the elimination of Israel). Participants were told to "target" small churches, and win the trust of church members by "looking and acting Christian". They were told to wear Western-style clothes, be well-groomed and speak nicely. "If someone sneezes, say God bless you. And always come bearing gifts, especially

---

27   Speaking on "A Question of Leadership", Panorama, BBC 1 (21 August 2005)

something from the Holy Land like holy water or rosary beads." They were advised to get involved with the church community. "Don't look down on the church ladies' clubs – join them."[28] This deliberate deception is part of *taqiyya*.

One of the ways in which *taqiyya* is manifested in the West today is the rewriting of history and in the mantra-like repetitive assertion that "Islam is peace". The Muslim version of history, as presented all too often in school textbooks as well as TV programmes and exhibitions, manages on the one hand to exclude all the negative aspects of Islam such as conquest, slavery and empire, and on the other hand to present Islam as being followed at ludicrously unlikely times and places. Thus Westerners are told that Islam arrived in Australia in the ninth century AD[29] and in North America before Christopher Columbus got there.[30] They are told that Napoleon Bonaparte was a Muslim, as was Offa the eighth century Saxon King of Mercia. It is even suggested that William Shakespeare followed a kind of Islamic mysticism.

Likewise the historical achievements of Islam in the arts and sciences are exaggerated, while the oppression of non-Muslim minorities and of women is minimised. The take-home message is that European civilisation is based on Islamic civilisation. The fact that Islamic civilisation itself drew heavily on the learning of Greek, Hindu and other cultures is underplayed, as is the fact that many of the individuals within the Muslim world who contributed most to the achievements of "Islamic" civilisation were actually *dhimmi*, i.e. the Jews and Christians living in the midst of the Muslims.

---

28   Reported by Roz Rothstein and Roberta Seid, "Terror Comes to Georgetown" in FrontPageMagazine.com (22 February 2006).
      http://frontpagemag.com/Articles/ReadArticle.asp?ID=21405 (viewed 24 February 2006)
29   *Islam in Brisbane*, issued by Brisbane City Council (2004), p.3
30   George Archibald, "Textbook on Arabs Removes Blunder" in *The Washington Times* (16 April 2004)

Islamic theology is often presented in the West in a way which conceals its faults and magnifies its virtues. This can be part of *da'wa* or simply a prudent tactic for creating a favourable image of the Muslim minority to the majority society. Non-Muslims tend to be vulnerable to this kind of propaganda because of their lack of knowledge about Islam. Four fallacies about the Islamic faith which are frequently heard in the West are as follows:

- *The word "Islam" means "peace".* In fact, it means "submission".

- *Islam is a religion of peace and there are many verses to prove this in the Qur'an.* There are indeed many peaceable verses in the Qur'an but they are abrogated by later-dated warlike verses. (See page 49.) Furthermore, it is essential to remember that the Qur'an is not the only source of Islamic law. The *hadith* are also very important, and they record many warlike words and examples. So the important question to ask is not "What does the Qur'an say?" but "What does the *shari'a* say?" This is very different from the situation in Christianity where the Bible alone is the ultimate source of doctrine. So arguments based solely on the content of the Qur'an can be misleading; it all depends how the Qur'an is interpreted in classical Orthodox Islam.

- *The Qur'an says: "If you kill one soul it is as if you killed all mankind."* These or similar words, often quoted to prove that Islam is only peaceable, are a misquote. The actual Qur'anic text runs: "If anyone killed a person not in retaliation of murder, or (and) to spread mischief in the land – it would be as if he killed all mankind" (sura 5, verse 32). The very next verse lists a selection of savage punishments for those who wage war against Allah and Muhammad and make "mischief" (or in some translations "corruption") in the land. These punishments include execution, crucifixion and amputation. The meaning of the verse depends on what is understood by "retaliation of murder" and "mischief in the land" i.e. on what justifies killing. Some Muslims interpret "mischief in the land" as meaning secularism, democracy and other non-Islamic values in a land. Some consider that "murder" includes the killing of Muslims in Iraq by British forces.

- *The Qur'an says: "There is no compulsion in religion," which proves that there is full religious liberty in Islam.* The quote is accurate (from sura 2, verse 256) but the interpretation is a special one for Westerners. The normal Muslim interpretation of this verse is that Muslims will not be forced to fulfil all their religious duties, it is up to them whether they do so or not. This verse has nothing to say about freedom of conscience, which is severely restricted in Islam, given that Muslims are not permitted to leave their faith. In any case, it is an early verse, so many consider it to have been abrogated by later verses.

Curses

Sometimes cursing prayers against Christians (and – even more so – against Jews) are used at Friday prayers. The practice of cursing Christians, Jews and infidels in general (i.e. non-Muslims) is based on verses in the Qur'an.

> Verily, those who conceal the clear proofs, evidences and the guidance, which We have sent down, after We have made it clear for the people in the Book, they are the ones cursed by Allah and cursed by the cursers.[31]

---

31   Sura 2, verse 159

And the Jews say: 'Uzair (Ezra) is the son of Allah, and the Christians say: Messiah is the son of Allah. That is their saying with their mouths, resembling the saying of those who disbelieved aforetime. Allah's Curse be upon them, how they are deluded away from the truth![32]

It is also based on examples in the *hadith* such as:.

... Allah's Apostle further said, "May Allah curse the Jews, for Allah made the fat (of animals) illegal for them, yet they melted the fat and sold it and ate its price.[33]

On his death-bed Allah's Apostle put a sheet over his face and when he felt hot, he would remove it from his face. When in that state (of putting and removing the sheet) he said, "May Allah's Curse be on the Jews and the Christians for they build places of worship at the graves of their prophets."...[34]

Some Muslims are uncomfortable with the idea of cursing non-Muslims indiscriminately. A *fatwa* issued by "a group of muftis" on 30th October 2003 addressed this concern and said that it was only permissible to curse non-Muslims who were at war with Muslims or seeking to harm them. A *fatwa* from a scholar at Al-Azhar University, Cairo, the leading centre of Sunni Islam, said that such prayers were part of *jihad* and resisting oppression or injustice.[35]

Some examples of cursing prayers are as follows:

O Allah, destroy the *kuffar* [infidels i.e. non-Muslims] who are trying to prevent people from following Your path, who deny Your Messengers and who do not believe in Your promise (the Day of Judgement). Make them disunited, fill

32   Sura 9, verse 30
33   Sahih Al-Bukhari Hadith 3.438, narrated by Jabir bin Abdullah
34   Sahih Al-Bukhari Hadith 4.660, narrated by Aisha and Ibn Abbas
35   www.islamonline.net/servlet/Satellite?pagename=IslamOnline-English-Ask_Scholar/FatwaE/FatwaE&cid=1119503545224 (viewed 17 January 2006)
36   "Night Prayer During Ramadhan (Al-Qiyaam or Taraweeh)" issued by Khalid Bin al-Walid Mosque, Toronto, Canada
     www.khalidmosque.com/en/modules.php?op=modload&name=Sections&file=index&req=viewarticle&artid=130&page=1 (viewed 17 January 2006)

their hearts with terror and send Your wrath and punishment against them, O God of Truth.[36]

O God, destroy the Jews and their supporters and the Christians and their supporters and followers. O God, destroy the ground under their feet, instil fear in their hearts, and freeze the blood in their veins. (From the Grand Mosque in Sanaa, Yemen)

O God, destroy the Jews and their supporters, including the crusaders and some so-called Muslims. O God, use your power against them. (From the Umar Bin-al-Khattab Mosque in Doha, Qatar)

O God, destroy the Jews and Americans for they are within your power. O God, show them a black day. O God, shake the ground under their feet, weaken them, hang their flags at half mast, down their planes, and drown their ships. (From the Abu-Hanifah al-Nu'man mosque in Baghdad, Iraq)

O Allah, perish America, Christians and their allies. O God, destroy their homes, widow their women and make their children orphans! O God, destroy all the Jews and Christians. (From a mosque in an Arab country)[37]

Night prayer during Ramadan appears to be a time when cursing prayers are quite often used.[38] Christians who do a special month of prayer for Muslims during Ramadan should be aware of this spiritual dimension. At the very least they should be sure to pray for the protection for themselves, for unity amongst Christians and for a strong faith, remembering that death, destruction, disunity and fear are the main things which the cursing prayers ask for.

---

37   Islam Online – Fatwa, Date of Reply: 30/Oct/2003,
      http://www.islamonline.net/servlet/Satellite?pagename=IslamOnline-English-
      Ask_Scholar/FatwaE/FatwaE&cid=1119503545224 (viewed 17 January 2006)
38   See for example no. 17 in instructions for "Night Prayer During Ramadan" from the
      Khalid Bin Al-Walid Mosque, Toronto www.khalidmosque.com/en/
      modules.php?op=modload&name=Sections&file=index&req=viewarticle&artid=130&
      page=1 (viewed 17 January 2006)

Curses are often included in the *qunoot* prayers offered after regular morning prayers in mosques whenever the *umma* seems to be experiencing trouble, for example natural disaster, plague or war. One pattern for such a prayer is:

> O Allah, let Your curse be on those unbelievers who prevent people from treading Your path, who reject Your prophets and fight Your chosen ones. O Allah, make difficult their plans, shake their feet and give them such punishment which is not turned away from a sinning people.[39]

Diversity in Islam

The complexity of Islam, and the diversity of opinion within it, cannot be over-emphasised.

Major divisions

Following Muhammad's death in 632, he was succeeded in sequence by four of his most trusted companions – Abu Bakr, Umar, Uthman and Ali, the "Rightly guided Caliphs". The three major groupings within Islam arose from disagreements about the line of succession.

Sunnis

The Sunnis held that any suitable person from Muhammad's tribe of Quraysh was eligible to be elected as caliph. Sunni empires and states have dominated the Muslim world throughout its history and Sunnis comprise the great majority of Muslims today (at least 80%).

In the last two centuries Sunni Islam has become increasingly dominated by Wahhabism, a puritanical movement which originated in the Arabian peninsula. Wahhabism is being promoted worldwide with Saudi money. Wahhabis reject all cultural manifestations such as folk

---

39   "Qunoot - E - Naazilah", http://www.communities.ninemsn.com.au/AMHCY/howtopray.
msnw?action=get_message&mview=0&ID_Message=592&LastModified=467541483707
5584617 (viewed 17 January 2006). Jamiatul Ulama (Kwa Zulu Natal), Council of Muslim
Theologians, issued by Al Jamiat Publications, Durban, South Africa
www.jamiat.org.za/qunoot.html (viewed 17 January 2006)

Islam (see pages 42- 43). They reject the standard schools of *shari'a* and later developments in Islam and demand a return to the early model of Muhammad and his Companions and their followers, the first three generations in Islam. They limit religious authority to the Qur'an and *hadith* inter-preted in a literalist manner.

Shi'as
The Shi'as, who today comprise almost 20% of all Muslims, believe that only Ali, Muhammad's cousin and son-in-law, and Ali's male descendants are the legitimate successors to Muhammad. Their hopes were frustrated when Ali's reign ended with his assassination and his son Hussein was killed whilst seeking to regain the caliphate.

Shi'a Islam touches the emotions much more than does Sunni Islam; self-denial and martyrdom are strongly emphasised.

The Shi'as are today a majority in Iran, Iraq, Azerbaijan and Bahrain. There are significant Shi'a minorities in Yemen, Lebanon, some other Gulf states and the Indian subcontinent. Shi'a Islam has split into numerous sects including the Isma'ilis (who once established the magnificent Fatimid Empire in Egypt, but are now a scattered minority, led mainly by the Agha Khan). In Turkey there is a significant Shi'a minority, the Alevis, who revere Ali as an incarnation of God.

Kharijis
The third group of early Muslims, the Kharijis, rejected both Sunni and Shi'a claims, arguing that the position of caliph should be open to any suitable Muslim, no matter what their tribe or family. The Kharijis were a constant source of rebellion and civil war against mainstream Islam for several centuries. They were finally crushed and virtually exterminated so that only tiny remnants,

now peaceful, survive today in Oman and North Africa, where they are called respectively Ibadis and Mzabis.

Sufism[40]

There are many individual Muslims, both Sunni and Shi'a, who hunger for an inner spiritual reality. They may seek this in Sufism, that is, Islamic mysticism, which is very much concerned with the sincerity of intention. A main goal of Sufism is mystical union with God. It also stresses the intercessory power of Muslim saints.

Amongst Sufism's distinctives are the importance of knowledge of God's commands and remembrance (*zikr* or *dhikr*) of him by devotional chanting etc. The goal of *dhikr* is purification of the heart, producing in it the love of God and a consciousness of his greatness as well as peace, fulfilment and contentment. Sufism focuses on the hereafter and on seeking divine approval, rather than on material blessing in the present world. It emphasises both an inner discipline and also conformity to the Islamic code of social conduct. Sufism can also involve the concept of the "warrior saint" and Sufis have been active in rebellion and militant dissent.

Sufism is rejected by Wahhabis as not truly Islamic; they consider it theologically suspect and some of its doctrines even blasphemous. It is, however, a type of Islam which appeals particularly to Westerners. Many Western converts to Islam are Sufis.

Folk Islam

Islam is not just built on theological premises and the five pillars but also undergirded by culture. The cultural aspects include pre-Islamic Arabian culture as well as accretions of the cultures of the various other peoples

---

40   An excellent work on Sufism is P. Lewis, *Pirs, Shrines and Pakistani Islam* (Rawalpindi, Christian Study Centre, 1985)

who became Muslim as Islam expanded.[41] Together with Qur'anic and *hadith* passages about evil spiritual powers (especially *jinn*) and aspects of Sufism, these constitute "folk Islam". It is widespread among the poor and uneducated, but impacts all levels of Muslim society, running in parallel with orthodox Islam.

Folk Islam is primarily concerned with using spiritual powers to meet felt needs such as healing of illness, exorcism and protection from evil *jinn*. Much time and energy are devoted to trying to influence spiritual powers in one's favour, using amulets, vows, curses, invocations of God's name, and the placing of Qur'anic verses around the home or person, etc. God is considered far away and unknowable, but Muslim saints are seen as accessible protectors from evil, intercessors with God, and sources of supernatural power. Their tombs and shrines are places of pilgrimage and prayer. A very important aspect of folk Islam is the veneration of Muhammad, who is considered a powerful intercessor.[42]

Other factors
As well as the theology of the caliphate succession there are other factors that divide the Muslim world. Ethnicity is one such factor, as seen in the Middle East where Sunni Kurds have fought against Sunni Turks and Arabs for decades, or in Nigeria where an ethnic Yoruba Muslim may even feel more loyalty to a Yoruba Christian than to an ethnic Hausa Muslim.

In other parts of the Islamic world, where social structures are largely feudal in nature such as Pakistan, Yemen or Oman, society may be divided into castelike stratifications. In many societies in Africa and Asia, Muslim and non-Muslim alike are divided by tribe, clan and kin

---

41   Bill Musk *The Unseen Face of Islam* (Eastbourne, MARC, 1989) pp.229-231
42   Bill Musk *The Unseen Face of Islam* pp.231-236

group. However, the ideal is considered to be Arabic Islam because the final revelation was given to Muhammad, an Arab, and is recorded in heaven in Arabic.

Trends in contemporary Islam

Another analysis divides Muslims into three very broad categories representing different contemporary trends.

Conservatives

The overwhelming majority of the world's Muslims fall into this category. They are traditional and broadly orthodox in their beliefs, but also may be fairly nominal in their practice, doing little beyond fasting in Ramadan and praying when they can. Like most people of any religion, everyday realities such as raising families and finding work are of more immediate concern than the demands of their faith. Many will know little of Islam beyond the broad outlines, but these they would hold to with a strong conviction. (A comparison could be made with Christian Europe in the Middle Ages, where virtually everyone firmly believed in Christianity, but for most it was not the defining focus or concern of their daily lives.) However, when confronted by a situation which throws their faith into stark relief most Muslims in this category would clearly identify themselves with a conservative Islamic position. Thus they would not engage in violence themselves but might well sympathise with and even finance Osama bin Laden and other militants whom they see as championing the Muslim world against its Western oppressors.

Broadly speaking this group is undergoing change in the direction of becoming more observant and more devout, a change which is manifested both in Muslim-majority contexts and in Muslim-minority contexts. Furthermore it is gradually losing members to both ends of the spectrum, that is, to the radicals (Islamists) and, to a lesser extent, the liberals.

Islamists
These are radically active Muslims who are dedicated to transforming society to conform with *shari'a*. They adhere to a very rigid and austere form of Islam and apply literally all aspects of classical Islamic teaching including the expansion of *Dar al-Islam* through military struggle. This category is much smaller than the conservatives but is growing due to the increasing radicalisation of conservatives.

Islamists have a political agenda in their own home countries as well as in the West, with long-term strategies for the Islamisation of the world. Some Islamists are willing to use "democratic methods" in the process of turning democracies into Islamic states. Other Islamists would be willing to engage in terror as a means to intimidate and conquer.

Liberals
Very much a minority and far smaller in number than the radicals, Muslims in this category have adapted their faith to conform to modernity. They are usually well-educated and often live or have lived in the West. They accept without qualification the Western understanding of concepts such as human rights, democracy, equality and freedom of thought and speech, separation of state from religion, and are willing to engage in criticism of their own faith, culture and communities in support of these concepts. If Islamists can be said to believe that the modern world should adapt to Islam, modernists can be said to believe that Islam should adapt to the modern world. Some of these liberal intellectuals have been subject to huge pressure and threats from other Muslims to try

to make them change their position. (See page 62 for some examples.)

Most liberals are not particularly devout, indeed many are so secularised that they have only a vestigial faith and could more properly be described as agnostic. Increasingly they have "privatised" their faith and cut themselves off from the formal practices of classical Islam as well as from Islam's past. Some have even rejected Islam altogether and embraced beliefs like atheism while remaining culturally Muslim.

There are also Muslims who are liberal in their outlook but conservative in their theology. Muslims of this kind had some influence on the wider Muslim community during the colonial and early post-colonial periods. (A prominent example would be Muhammad Ali Jinnah, the founder of Pakistan.) More recently however, with the growing influence of Islamists and extremist Muslims, their influence has waned. This position might be classified as "moderate", although that is a very confusing term used to cover a wide range of different stances. The important question with Muslim liberals is always how far they embrace Western secular values, especially the separation of state and religion, the value of the individual, freedom of choice and freedom of conscience.

Understanding what is happening in the Muslim world today

The European colonial period had a numbing effect on Islamic culture and thought. The once glorious civilisations of the Islamic world had so clearly been conquered and surpassed by Christian Europe in so many areas, and this prompted a degree of reflection and the adoption of Western ideals and concepts. Thus in the immediate post-colonial years the states that emerged in the Islamic world were almost all Western-style nation-states with Western-based constitutions and legislation. However since the 1970s this has begun to change with increasing rapidity. Many Muslim leaders, reformers and intellectuals are feeling that borrowed ideals like nationalism, socialism, communism and capitalism have failed the Muslim world. They are increasingly rejecting the West, returning to traditional and literal applications of Islamic teaching, and looking for answers within their own historical and religious tradition. Various catalysts such as the huge financial investment by Saudi Arabia and other oil-rich Gulf states in promoting Islam, the Iranian revolution of 1979, the *jihad* in Afghanistan during the 1980s and more recently the wars of the early years of the twenty-first century in Afghanistan and Iraq have accelerated this process. A revival and resurgence is taking place within Islam today which will have enormous influence on the future of the whole world.

2

COMPARING ISLAM WITH CHRISTIANITY

Although Islam and Christianity have certain points of doctrine in common, such as a belief in one God, revealed scriptures and the Day of Judgement, there is an enormous difference between them in the crucial areas of understanding of God's nature, Christ and salvation, as well as in many other areas affecting daily lives, attitudes and worldviews. While they share some beliefs, on the most important ones their understandings are completely different.

The Archbishop of Canterbury has suggested that it is better to look first at the theological differences between two faiths before trying to work together.

> Once we are clearer about the nature and scope of religious disagreement, we are actually more rather than less likely to develop a respectful and collaborative practice in inter-faith relations.[43]

The real difference between Christianity and Islam lies in the core issues of their sacred writings and the persons of their founders. Christians have frequently in their long history departed from Christ's teachings and perpetrated cruelties against Jews, Muslims and heretics. However, when returning to their source scriptures they come face to face with the person of Christ and the Gospel of love and forgiveness he preached, as well as his

---

43   Most Rev. Rowan Williams, "Christian Theology and Other Faiths" (paper given at Birmingham University, 11 June 2003)

atoning death and supreme example of humility, service, suffering and non-violence. When Muslims return to their original sources, they have a very different encounter. The later dated verses of the Qur'an, revealed to Muhammad in Medina, contain much that is intolerant and belligerent. According to the most commonly followed doctrine of abrogation, later verses supersede earlier (more peaceable) verses dating from his days in Mecca. Muslims also meet Muhammad, whose words and actions, recorded in the *hadith*, give many clear examples of aggression, warmongering, even what in modern terminology appear to be assassination, torture and genocide. Some Muslims will argue that these actions were for a particular context only, but the fact remains that they occurred. Setting up Muhammad as the supreme example in every aspect of his words and actions, necessitates transforming his vices into virtues. This is the real cause of the contradictions so prevalent in Islamic societies and Islamic history, especially on issues relating to *jihad*, the treatment of women, and the contempt shown to non-Muslims.

Having made this comparison, it should be added that another vital difference is the relative importance of the founder and of the scriptures. The Christian faith is ultimately a relationship with a Person, but Islam is focused on the authority of a book.

God, the Trinitarian loving Father
The important question is not whether Muslims and Christians believe in "the same God", but what they understand his character to be. Christians understand the nature of God by looking into the face of Christ who revealed God to humanity. They believe God's primary attribute is love and call him Father. Christians also believe in a God who responds to humans' repentance and faith.

Islam stresses God's transcendence. He is so "other" that he cannot be adequately described in human language, neither can he enter into the experiences of humanity, so he cannot suffer. An individual's relation to God is best described as slave to master. The Islamic teachings on predestination encourage passivity and fatalism, as no one can change what God has ordained.

Christians believe that Jesus is God's Son not in the carnal sense, but in the sense that he has the Father's eternal nature and attributes. The Trinity, although a divine mystery, is clearly attested in scripture and is the basis for our personal relationship with God. Human love and relationships are rooted in the love and relationships within the divine Trinity. Muslims deny the Trinity, which they understand in terms of God having sexual relations with Mary who then bore Jesus. They state categorically that God can have no son, and they view the Trinity as blasphemy, a pagan belief in three gods.

Jesus Christ
Christians view Christ as the second person of the Godhead, the Lord who is to be worshipped and adored. Christ's incarnation and substitutionary death on the cross are God's redemptive plan from all eternity, forming the basis of God's offer of free salvation to all who believe.

Islam rejects Christ's deity[44] and Sonship,[45] and there is reference to this in the first half of the Islamic creed which states: "There is no god but God..." Although Islam reveres Jesus as a sinless[46] prophet[47] and miracle-

---

44   Sura 4, verse 171; sura 5, verse 116; sura 3, verse 59
45   Sura 19, verses 34-35; sura 6, verses 101-106; sura 112
46   Sura 19, verse 19. A *hadith* says: "The Prophet said, 'When any human being is born, Satan touches him at both sides of the body with his two fingers, except Jesus, the son of Mary, whom Satan tried to touch, but failed, for he touched the placenta-cover instead.'" (Sahih Al-Bukhari Hadith 4.506, narrated by Abu Huraira)
47   Sura 4, verse 171; sura 33, verse 7

worker,[48] he is placed only in the second of heaven's seven levels. Islam accepts the virgin birth[49] and Christ's second coming (albeit as a Muslim)[50], but it denies Christ's crucifixion[51] and therefore his atoning sacrifice, and resurrection, claiming that someone else was crucified in his place. Islam thus denies the very heart of the Christian faith.

Christians believe that Christ is God's final revelation to mankind but Muslims believe that a later and final revelation was added when the message of the Qur'an was given to Muhammad. This is the thought behind the second half of the Islamic creed: "... and Muhammad is his messenger." The Islamic creed is in fact aimed at denying Christianity, especially the finality of Christ, and asserting the supremacy of Islam.

Mankind and the fall
Christians believe in mankind's inherent sinfulness which makes humans unable to redeem themselves. They are cast on God's mercy and grace in Christ. Through the work of the Holy Spirit lives and characters are transformed, which in turn affects community and society. Muslims deny the sinfulness of mankind due to the fall, viewing human nature as inherently good, though weak. There is thus no original sin and no necessity for God's intervention in redemption. Most Muslims have a utopian view of the perfectibility of man given the right environment (i.e. under *shari'a*), making checks and balances in politics and society unnecessary.

Christians see all humans as equal in worth because all are created in God's image (*imago dei*). Non-Christians are

---

48   Sura 5, verse 110
49   Sura 3, verse 45-47
50   Sura 19, verses 33-34 Muslims interpret these ambiguous verses as a prediction of his
      second coming, not of his resurrection. See also sura 43, verse 61 which is interpreted in
      the same way
51   Sura 4, verse 157

to be served in love and offered the Gospel freely. They are to be treated as equals and are not to suffer any disabilities because of their religion, race or gender. Islam finds very offensive the view that humans are created in God's image. Muslims therefore do not consider that there is an innate equality of all people, the basis of human rights. Instead, Islam sets up a rigid social order, defined in the *shari'a*, which differentiates between Muslim and non-Muslim, and between male and female. Each category is treated differently: non-Muslims are of less value than Muslims and women of less value than men. Obligatory duties are emphasised rather than inherent rights.

Salvation and grace
For Christians, salvation means forgiveness of sins, acceptance into God's family, and the certainty of eternal life in heaven in God's presence. Christians believe salvation is an undeserved free gift of God's grace offered on the basis of Christ's atoning death.

In Islam salvation is through good works and religious rituals and there is no need for God's intervention in grace and atonement. On the Day of Judgement all one's good and bad deeds will be weighed in the divine scales. Muslims have no assurance of salvation as no one can predict whether their good deeds will outweigh their sins, or indeed what God may choose to do in his omnipotence. Paradoxically, because God does as he wills, the outcome of God's judgement is unpredictable: he will save or condemn whom he will regardless of their conduct. No one can be sure of their eternal destiny, except martyrs.

Mission

Christianity is a missionary religion with a mandate to preach the Gospel to all the world. However, it stresses the free choice of individuals in their response to the Gospel. The emphasis is on the individual's – not the community's – choice to love God and to follow Christ. Christian mission should involve neither coercion nor deception. All should be done with openness, integrity and transparency. Christ calls us to be as wise as serpents but as gentle as doves. Christian mission should be done with vulnerability and the giving of oneself, a spirit that is free from arrogance and pride, being constrained by the love of Jesus. This is not to deny the sad fact that Christians have not always lived up to this teaching and that at times the Church has enforced conversions and severely punished heresy and apostasy. Similarly missionaries have sometimes used methods that have amounted to deceit in their eagerness to win converts.

Islam is also a missionary religion and all Muslims have the obligation to witness to their faith, win converts and Islamise other communities. Muslims use many methods for this *da'wa*, including efforts at the gradual Islamisation of non-Muslim societal structures. While freedom exists to propagate Islam in the West, most Muslim states severely restrict Christian mission or completely forbid it. Indeed Christian mission is one of the three greatest grievances which Muslims hold against the West, the other two being the Crusades and colonialism.

Theological understanding of Islam

From the above comparisons it is clear that it is impossible for a Christian to regard Muhammad as a legitimate prophet in line with the biblical revelation or to believe that his message was authentic revelation. It is alarming to note that the General Council of the United Church of Canada will be considering in August 2006 a proposal to acknowledge formally the prophetic witness of Muhammad. Any statement of this kind, no matter how cunningly phrased, would be seen by Muslims as confirmation of their position. Islam should therefore not be viewed as a brother monotheistic faith like Judaism with which Christians have a special relationship. The idea of three sibling "Abrahamic" faiths is an Islamic concept, not a Christian one. Rather Islam should be viewed in the same bracket as Christian heresies, Jehovah's Witnesses or Mormons. To accept the Muslims' concept of three "Abrahamic" faiths is effectively to agree with the Islamic teaching on replacement – Judaism was replaced by Christianity which was in turn replaced by Islam. The ultimate logic of this would be for all Christians to convert to Islam.

Christians must not let themselves forget the basic truth that it is faith in Jesus Christ which God is looking for, not faith in general. In a secular, materialistic culture, it is tempting to think that Muslims and Christians can be allies against the overwhelming godless hedonism which surrounds them both.[52] But Christians must always bear in mind that Islam denies the heart of the Christian faith, and that its very creed – which resounds from minarets five times a day as the *muezzin* calls Muslims to prayer – was formulated to deny the deity of Christ and the finality of His revelation. When the *muezzin* calls "There is no god but God" he is saying that Jesus is not God, and when he adds that "Muhammad is his messenger" he is saying that Jesus has been superseded by Muhammad.

---

52   For example, Peter Kreeft, *Ecumenical Jihad: Ecumenism and the Culture War* (San Francisco: Ignatius Press, 1996). It is interesting how the word "ecumenical" has broadened its meaning from "belonging to the entire Christian Church" to include other faiths, especially Islam.

3

ISSUES

There are numerous issues related to Islam and especially its presence in the West which Christians should be aware of. Given that Islam does not separate the sacred from the secular or religion from society, the presence of Islam is bound to involve Islamic aspirations for the reconstruction of society according to Islamic values.

Under the guise of preventing Islamophobia, of fighting racism and of struggling for equal rights in a multiracial society, Islamic lobby groups in the West pressurise governments, parliaments, media, schools, academia and the legal systems of their adopted countries to move Western societies in the direction of expanding their Judaeo-Christian basis to include Islam, thus creating a society with a Judaeo-Christian-Islamic basis. From this point they move on gradually to seek for Islam privileges above any other religion or faith community. A stage in this process is the Warsaw Declaration of the Council of Europe, agreed in May 2005, where, as a result of Turkish lobbying, Islamophobia was for the first time listed alongside anti-Semitism as an example of religious intolerance and discrimination to be condemned and eradicated. No other kinds of religious discrimination were mentioned by name.

There is also an argument presented by some Muslim strategists that in order to avoid cultural conflicts the "moderate Muslims" and the "moderate Christians" should unite against the "extremists" in both camps. The suggestion is that both kinds of extremists are a danger to communal harmony. This is a very subtle twisting of issues, since it negates the huge difference between Muslim extremists (who call for the murder of unbelievers, and denounce freedom, democracy etc.) and conservative Christians (who do not do any of those things). The increasingly frequent phenomenon of equating fundamentalist Islam with fundamentalist Christianity is extremely misleading. Fundamentalist Christianity is ultimately based on love and on being conformed to Christ; it rejects the principle of violence, unlike fundamentalist Islam.

Legal protection
Some Western states have adopted legislation that seeks to protect religions (as opposed to their followers) by prohibiting incitement to religious hatred or the vilification of religion. This has in effect limited the freedom of expression so prized by Western democracies. Muslims are quick to seize upon any available legislation to try to attack any perceived slighting of Islam.

Italian journalist Oriana Fallaci has faced legal proceedings in Switzerland (2002), France (2003) and Italy (2005) for her book *La Rabbia e L'Orgoglio* (Rage and Pride) which warned of the danger posed by Islamism to Western civilisation and freedoms and accepted the concept of a clash of cultures between Islam and the West. Her opponents included both Islamic groups and anti-racism groups. She now lives in the USA.

In September 2002 Michel Houellebecq, a French philosopher, was taken to court by the Paris Mosque and the Muslim World League for incitement to racial hatred. In one of his novels he had depicted a woman being killed by Islamic terrorists. He had also described the Qur'an as appalling. The court cleared him of all charges on 22nd

October 2002, agreeing that his remarks were a judgment on a religion, not an incitement to hatred.

In the Australian state of Victoria, two Christian pastors were found guilty in December 2004 because they had made statements critical of Islam at a seminar intended for Christians. The complaints were made by the Islamic Council of Victoria under the state's Racial and Religious Tolerance Act (2001) and the section which the two pastors were found to have breached was a ban on inciting "hatred against, serious contempt for or revulsion or severe ridicule of" another person or group on the basis of religious belief or activity. This Act can apparently be used by Muslims to stifle all criticism of Islam or Muslims. It is ironic, to say the least, that a law which was intended to promote tolerance has, in a few short years, created intolerance and a culture of fear.

In some Muslim states *shari'a*-based blasphemy and apostasy laws are used to intimidate Muslims in order to prevent them from expressing reformist and liberal ideas on Islam. Non-Muslims also are often prosecuted under these laws which carry harsh punishments. Following international Muslim protests over cartoons of Muhammad published in the West (see pages 63-64) the Organisation of the Islamic Conference[53] called for the adoption of legislations to protect the sanctity of religions and prophets.

Education

Muslims are making use of Western education systems to present a favourable image of Islam to the West. Many of the Muslim educators and institutions approached by Western governments and public bodies for advice are influenced by Islamism; they will therefore present a sanitised

---

53   The Organisation of the Islamic Conference is an inter-governmental grouping of 57 Muslim states dedicated to promoting the cause of Islam in the world.

view of Islam, ignoring elements deemed objectionable in the West, while sometimes denigrating and minimising other Muslim streams they oppose.

In a process which might be called the Islamisation of knowledge, Muslims are trying to influence school curricula and to gain input into the process of rewriting the textbooks used for religious education and history. A version of Islam is presented that ignores its more violent aspects and the historical atrocities committed in its name. The guidelines offered are also silent about the inferior position of women and non-Muslims in Islamic societies as outlined by *shari'a*.[54]

The climate of accusations of Islamophobia is making many teachers in the UK so anxious to avoid criticism that they are unable to teach an objective view of Islam. The result is a tendency to teach Islam more sympathetically than Christianity. So British school-children are studying Christianity from a critical basis but are often taught Islam completely uncritically. Some teaching methods include asking the students (even of primary school age) to pretend to be a Muslim and try to enter into a Muslim's thought processes. Young children are also being taken to visit mosques.[55]

Another issue is that of Islamic schools, where Muslim children are taught a very strict, classical understanding of their faith. The London School of Islamics has called for all state schools with a majority of Muslim pupils (which would include many Church of England schools) to be designated Muslim community schools and put under

---

54   See Gilbert T. Sewell *Islam and the Textbooks*. A report of the American Textbook Council (New York: American Textbook Council, 2003). A recent examination of a draft for the teaching of Islam in state primary schools in the UK, prepared for a regional Standing Advisory Council on Religious Education, revealed similar tendencies.

55   When Muslim school-children are taken to visit churches, they are often allowed a Muslim adviser to accompany them and explain everything to them from an Islamic point of view. It is doubtful whether Christian children going to a mosque would ever be allowed to have a Christian with them to guide their understanding.

the control of Muslim educational trusts or charities.[56]

Treatment of women[57]

Some Muslim women (primarily of the secularised Western elites) enjoy equal status with men, but the majority suffer legal and cultural discrimination and restrictions on personal freedoms. This is especially severe in countries that operate *shari'a* courts in addition to the secular court system and even more so in countries which do not have civil/secular courts at all.[58] Women have fewer rights than men in divorce and custody cases. As mentioned above, the value of a woman's testimony in a law court is worth less than that of a man and she gets less compensation for the same injury. In some countries women need their husband's permission to work or to travel abroad. Child marriages, forced marriages, female genital mutilation, polygamy, rape, honour killings and violent abuse by husbands are still fairly widespread. Not every item in this list is part of classical Islam, but Islam's general attitude towards women creates a climate which allows the other abuses to flourish unchecked. While the Taliban regime in Afghanistan was an extreme example of repression of women, UN and other human rights organisations have consistently reported on gross violations of the human rights of women in Muslim states.[59]

Some Muslim women are campaigning for a reinterpretation of *shari'a* rules on the status of women, but it is an uphill struggle which has made little impact so far. Ayyan Hirsi Ali, a Somali political scientist living in the

---

56 Iftikhar Ahmad, London School of Islamics "Muslim Schools" paper circulated by e-mail (30 June 2003)

57 For a detailed study of the situation of Muslim women living in the West, see Rosemary Sookhdeo, *Secrets Behind the Burqa: Islam, Women and the West* (Pewsey: Isaac Publishing, 2004)

58 See, for example, "Memorandum on Reform of the Islamic Family Laws and the Adminstration of Justice in the Syariah System in Malaysia" (Sisters in Islam, 2000)

59 See for example "Crime or Custom? Violence Against Women in Pakistan," Human Rights Watch, 1999. Also Joe Stork, "Human Rights Watch and the Muslim World", ISIM Newsletter, 2 March 1999, http://www.isim.nl/newsletter/2/

Netherlands, had to go into hiding in 2002 after receiving a barrage of hate mail and death threats from Muslims following a live debate on Dutch TV in which she accused Islam of treating women shoddily, and conservative Muslim groups of covering up cases of domestic violence and child abuse. Ms Hirsi Ali also condemned the government's support for programmes promoting multiculturalism which she claimed help keep Muslim women isolated from Dutch society.

It is striking that the cause of women in Islam has not been widely taken up in the UK. The traditional treatment of women and girls is perceived to be a part of Islamic culture and therefore above criticism, even if such treatment would be considered abuse in other contexts. The Sharia Council of Darul Uloom London has issued a set of rules on divorce and re-marriage which clearly envisage the possibility of pre-pubescent girls being married.[60] It is surprising that this has not provoked a furore.

Implementation of shari'a

Western colonial rulers partially dismantled the *shari'a* establishment in many of the Muslim countries they governed, replacing it to some extent with Western-style codes of law. However, since independence, many Muslim states have reintroduced parts of *shari'a* or have even designated it the source of their legislation. In Saudi Arabia it is regarded as the constitution, while in Iran it is the sole source of the legal system. Muslim groups seeking the reform of *shari'a* have gradually been marginalised.

---

60   Instructions are given on how long a woman must wait after divorce before marrying again. The ruling is that she must wait for three menstrual cycles, but in the case of a girl who has not yet started menstruation, she must wait three months. Sharia Council "Terms and Conditions for Talak or Divorce" at http://www.darululoomlondon.co.uk/sharia.htm (viewed 8 January 2004)

Whether or not *shari'a* is officially applied in any particular country at present, the long history of Muslims living under *shari'a* has ensured that the attitudes behind it are still prevalent amongst Muslims in all parts of the globe. The demand for the reintroduction of *shari'a* is a major platform of many Islamist movements. Even in the UK there is a creeping Islamisation which amounts to a *de facto* application of *shari'a*. Examples include the introduction of *shari'a*-compliant mortgages and pensions, and the provision of *halal* food in schools, prisons and hospitals. The Metropolitan Police now permit Muslim police officers to wear turbans. There have been calls for the legalisation of polygamy, this being presented as a basic human right for Muslim men. A London-based Sharia Council has already been mentioned and this is only one of many *shari'a* councils and *shari'a* courts operating informally in the UK to deal with divorce and other family disputes for the Muslim community.[61]

The resurgence of Islam has been accompanied by greatly increased violence against non-Muslims in countries like Sudan, Nigeria and Indonesia. This results from a revival of the *shari'a* concepts of *jihad* in its military sense and of the inferiority of non-Muslims.

The spread of rule by *shari'a* is without doubt part of the Islamist global strategy. One of the regions where this is being most actively pursued at present is sub-Saharan Africa, where Christianity and Islam are both growing rapidly. The introduction of *shari'a* effectively stakes a claim to Muslim superiority as opposed to Christian demands for the equality of all before the law. It also opens the door to the possibility of a Muslim minority taking control of the state, while shaping all of society in an Islamic mould.

---

61   For more examples of *shari'a* councils and *shari'a* courts see *Islam in Britain* (details in footnote 2, page 4) pp. 26-27

To allow Muslims in the West to be different in culture is one thing. To derive from this "right of difference" that they also have the right to be ruled by a different set of laws is unacceptable, since this would lead to the disintegration of the state and ultimately to the "Balkanisation" of Western society.

Media

Islam typically rejects any kind of negative comment and seeks to protect itself from criticism. In Pakistan the crime of "defiling the name of Muhammad" is seen as blasphemy and carries a mandatory death sentence. In 2005 a chemistry teacher at a school in Saudi Arabia was sentenced to 40 months in prison and 750 lashes because he spoke against jihadist violence, made fun of Muslim clerics' beards, and "favoured" Christians and Jews. In Egypt any criticism of Muhammad or the religion itself, no matter how scholarly, tends to be interpreted as apostasy and brings dire punishment. For example, Professor Nasr Hamid Abu-Zayd was declared an apostate by the Cairo Appeals Court in June 1995 and, as an apostate, was ordered to separate from his wife. (Dissolution of the marriage is one of the classical Islamic penalties for apostasy in addition to the death sentence.) The professor and his wife fled the country together. Abu-Zayd is a liberal-secularist academic who had held the chair of Islamic and Arabic Studies at Cairo University. In the course of his research he had studied the Qur'an and *hadith*; he had called the Qur'an a linguistic text, described it as a cultural product and denied its pre-existence on a tablet in heaven. In Sudan Mahmoud Muhammad Taha was executed for apostasy on 20th January 1985 because he refused to repent of his liberal views of Islam; he had been given just three days to repent, in accordance with *shari'a* rules.

Fearful of giving offence or being accused of Islam-ophobia, some sections of the Western media succumbed to a form of self-censorship in which Islam could not be criticised. Recently, however, it appears the pendulum may be swinging back the other way, with a growing willingness to express negative comments about certain aspects of Islam.

Muslim media in the West tend to blame Christianity for promoting colonialism, secularism and immorality as well as for being irrational and obscurantist. Christianity is presented as an ally of Orientalism and Judaism, which are considered by many Muslims to be engaged in a struggle to demean and destroy Islam.[62] Where left-wing anti-Christian attitudes, guilt for colonialism, political correctness and post-modern relativism predominate, it is easy for Muslim lobbyists to have considerable influence. Secular commentators often tend to denigrate Christ-ianity but to put Islam on a pedestal. An idealised Islam is presented and compared to the many short-comings of real-life Christianity.

It is noticeable also that blasphemies against the Lord Jesus Christ are a daily occurrence in the media, whereas the name of Muhammad is rarely mistreated, indeed it is increasingly prefixed with the title "The Prophet"[63]. Muhammad is respected but Christ is reviled.

On 30th September 2005 a leading Danish daily newspaper, *Jyllands-Posten*, published twelve cartoons of Muhammad, including one in which he was shown wearing a turban shaped like a bomb with a burning fuse. A Danish Muslim leader, Imam Ahmed Abu-Laban, said

---

62   Christianity is portrayed in the same way in many Muslim-majority contexts.

63   Christians wanting to refer to Muhammad more politely than simply "Muhammad" or to indicate which Muhammad is in question could use the phrase "the Islamic prophet Muhammad" or "Muhammad the prophet of Islam". This avoids implying that his prophethood is valid, as suggested by the media's phrase "the prophet Muhammad". Another option would be "Muhammad the founder of Islam".

the cartoons were inflicting mental torture on Muslims because they were blasphemous and insulting to Islam. The editor who commissioned the cartoons did so as a response to the self-censorship which he said had over-taken Europe since Dutch film-maker Theo van Gogh was murdered in 2004 by a radical Muslim for making a film critical of Islam's treatment of women. He wanted to test whether people would censor themselves for fear of provoking Muslims. Under the leadership of Egypt and Saudi Arabia, outraged Muslims across the world protested, as did ambassadors from Muslim countries, Arab foreign ministers, and the Organisation of the Islamic Conference. By early 2006 Muslims were rioting and attacking Christian minorities and Western embassies. Protests were also received from the United Nations, the Council of Europe and the European Union. Would any of these have prote-sted about a blasphemous depiction of the Lord Jesus Christ or indeed of a Hindu deity?

Politics

In Islam politics forms an integral part of religion and must serve the goal of protecting and promoting Islam, extending its dominion and implementing *shari'a* as far as possible. At the local and national level, Muslims in the West are carefully and patiently working to gain polit-ical power. In Germany radical Muslims are urging other Muslims to acquire German citizenship so that they will be eligible to vote. They would like a Muslim presence in all political parties so that they can maximise their influ-ence on the German political scene. In Britain, where many Muslims are from the Indian sub-continent, the strong clan networks known as *biraderis* make it easy for Muslim candidates to gain "block votes". The candidate's party allegiance or electoral platform is of virtually no relevance, as their entire *biraderi* will vote for them anyway because loyalty to the *biraderi* takes precedence. Muslim states have set up international organisations such as the Organisation of the Islamic Conference and the Muslim World League to coordinate global Muslim political goals, attitudes and responses. These also fund and direct a vast worldwide missionary [*da'wa*] effort.

Cruel shari'a punishments

According to *shari'a*, law courts must impose mandatory prescribed punishments (*hudud*, singular *hadd*) for certain specific crimes claimed to be committed against God and his rights. These include theft, highway robbery, adultery and fornication, false accusation of adultery and fornication, and drinking alcohol. Some Muslims also include apostasy from Islam as a *hadd* crime. In these cases the judge has no discretion in his sentencing, as the punishments are laid down in the Qur'an or *hadith*.

Although there are four main schools of *shari'a* law with slight differences between them, the following list of punishments is generally accepted:

- Theft: amputation of the hand at the wrist for a first offence. Further amputations follow for further offences.
- Highway robbery: loss of hands and feet. If the highway robbery involves murder, then the death sentence is imposed.
- Adultery: stoning to death
- Fornication by an unmarried person: 100 lashes
- False accusation of adultery or fornication: 80 lashes
- Drinking alcohol: 40 lashes
- Apostasy: death

While the severity of the punishments is theoretically tempered by strict rules of evidence, this has not stopped them being practised in certain modern states, for example, Saudi Arabia, Iran, Sudan, parts of Nigeria and Somalia, and Afghanistan when it was under Taliban rule.

Dhimmi

It cannot be denied that *shari'a* discriminates against non-Muslims, granting to Jews and Christians an inferior second-class status as *dhimmi*; this might be termed "institutional injustice". The literal meaning of *"dhimmi"* is "protected", because *dhimmi* are allowed to keep their faith and yet live. Other non-Muslims would according to classical Islam have to convert to Islam or be killed.

But *dhimmi*, although allowed to live, were not according to classical Islam entitled to equal status with Muslims. A host of rules and regulations affected their daily life, e.g. clothes, transport and places of worship. The thrust of these rules was to mark out the *dhimmi* visibly as non-Muslims, to show that they were considered inferior to Muslims, and to curtail their religious activities so that they did not impinge on the consciousness of the Muslim majority. This treatment of Jews and Christians is often described by Muslims as "tolerance"; it is important to realise that it does not imply equality or respect. A special poll tax called *jizya* was required from *dhimmi*. It was handed over with a humiliating public ceremony, in accordance with the teachings of the Qur'an that Jews and Christians should "pay the *jizya* with willing submission, and feel themselves subdued".[64]

While the full *dhimmi* system is not formally implemented by any modern Muslim-majority state, the legacy of hundreds of years of official scorn and discrimination towards non-Muslims has left its mark on most Muslim societies in terms of an enduring popular prejudice. This is the reason for much of the injustice

---

64   Sura 9, verse 29

suffered by Christian minorities in Muslim countries. It is the reason that so often police, judiciary, media, employers and teachers – not to mention angry mobs – can get away with anti-Christian behaviour, for the majority of society feels deep down that this is right and proper, part of Allah's plan for his creation.

In some countries there are even the remains of certain *dhimmi* regulations within twenty-first century legal systems. Islamic law courts function in some countries and these have an in-built bias against non-Muslims (and against women). In traditional Islamic law, the number of witnesses on each side of the case plays an important part in deciding the verdict. But Islam states that the testimony of a Christian is worth less than that of a Muslim. (Likewise, the testimony of a woman is worth less than that of a man.) So if a case hinges on the word of one Muslim against the word of one Christian, the Muslim must automatically be believed. This makes Christians very vulnerable when tried in Islamic courts.

The same mindset can also affect cases in non-Islamic courts, for example, when a Christian is accused by a Muslim under Pakistan's notorious "blasphemy law". Many malicious accusations have been made by Muslims against innocent Christians. The accuser knows that there is a mandatory death sentence for "defiling" the name of Muhammad but no penalty at all for false accusation. The accuser also knows that, as a Muslim, his words may be believed in preference to those of the Christian defendant.

A similar sliding scale governs the payment of compensation for injuries or death. In classical Islam, an injury suffered by a Christian (or a woman) receives a lower sum than the same injury suffered by a Muslim (or a man). Iranian Christians rejoiced in 2003 when for the first time a court granted the family of a murdered Christian as much compensation as would be given to the family of a murdered Muslim. Previously non-Muslims in Iran received only a fraction of what Muslims were entitled to.

Apostasy

For most contemporary Muslims across the spectrum of beliefs and ideologies, apostasy from Islam still carries shocking associations as an abhorrent sin. Theologically in Islam this is one of the few sins God cannot forgive. Even for some modernists and secularists apostasy has negative connotations of betrayal of one's community and rejection of one's heritage. This explains why so few Muslim voices are ever raised in defence of those accused of apostasy.

In Islamic jurisprudence, apostasy (*irtidad*) is linked to unbelief, blasphemy and heresy (all combined under the term *kufr*), which are sometimes used interchangeably. All are regarded as serious crimes, but there is unanimous consensus in all schools of *shari'a* that apostasy by a sane, adult male Muslim is punishable by death. Three out of five of the schools of *shari'a* also have the death penalty for women converts; the other two schools specify that the women should be imprisoned until they return to Islam. In practice the death penalty is not often implemented nowadays, but it is common to deprive apostates of their civil rights (the *shari'a* has detailed regulations for this kind of punishment for apostates, in addition to the death penalty). Even where there are no official penalties, those who leave Islam are more than likely to suffer harassment or rejection from family and community, sometimes even death.

Muslims too can be accused of unbelief, blasphemy and heresy and even apostasy if their beliefs are not mainstream. This is often what happens to liberals espousing a modernisation of the Islamic faith. (See page 62 for examples in Egypt and Sudan.) They may then be punished, murdered by zealous Islamists or even executed by the state. A significant feature of accusations of apostasy and blasphemy in Muslim-majority countries is the way they are often uncritically accepted as true by members of the police and judiciary, with little or no evidence required beyond the word of their accuser.

Jihad and the extension of Islamic territory
Calls for *jihad* in the sense of physical violence have been increasing with the growth of the Islamist movement. All Islamic terrorist groups justify their actions from the classical theology of *jihad*. They regard as permanent and literal the Qur'anic commands to fight Jews and Christians until they submit to Islamic dominance. Secular Muslim regimes are regarded as infidel for failing fully to implement *shari'a* and are therefore likewise to be fought by *jihad* until they are replaced by truly Islamic governments. Osama bin Laden's al-Qa'eda group and many similar organisations are inspired by this understanding of *jihad*.

In the West non-violent methods are being used to seek to gain Islamic sovereignty over geographical areas. The implementation of *shar'ia* in family matters and Muslim involvement in politics have already been mentioned. The extension of sacred space in the sense of the sanctification of physical territory is also seen in the name-changes forced by some British Muslims in the London Borough of Tower Hamlets who objected to saints' names and other Christian-sounding names in their area for parks, electoral wards etc.

Sufi Muslims may also "take" territory spiritually by means of a religious procession (*julus*) in which the name of Allah is chanted in various short phrases. The chanting (*dhikr*) is characteristic of Sufism. "This chanting not only purifies their hearts and souls, but also sacralises and 'Islamizes' the very earth, the buildings, the streets and neighborhoods through which they march." Such processions are held twice a year in ethnic areas of British cities including Birmingham, Manchester and London. They are also held in North America, for example, in Toronto and New York.[65][66]

---

65   Pnina Werbner, "Stamping the Earth with the Name of Allah: Zikr and the Sacralizing of Space among British Muslims" in Barbara Daly Metcalf (ed.), *Making Muslim Space in North America and Europe* (Berkeley, Los Angeles, London : University of California Press, 1996) pp.167-185. The quote is from p. 167.
66   Any Christians engaging in "prayer walks" in Muslim areas should be aware of this Islamic practice.

4

CHRISTIAN-MUSLIM RELATIONS

Having clarified the relationship between Christianity and Islam theologically and spiritually, and having highlighted some of the most pressing contemporary issues for Christians concerned about Islam, how are Christians actually to interact with and relate to Muslims?

Building friendships
A number of stumbling blocks and complications make the task of building friendships with Muslims rather more difficult than with other non-Christians. Christians may be puzzled or bewildered by the apparently capricious way in which Muslims relate to them. But often there is a theological rationale behind the Muslims' actions and reactions.

Many Muslims consider that it is displeasing to God for them to have Christians as friends. This is based on a verse in the Qur'an (sura 5, verse 51):

> O you who believe! Take not the Jews and the Christians as *Auliya'* (friends, protectors, helpers), they are but *Auliya'* of each other. And if any amongst you takes them (as *Auliya'*), then surely, he is one of them.

There is a *hadith* which even forbids Muslims from greeting Christians, but fortunately there are few Muslims who take this literally.

Allah's Messenger (peace be upon him) said: Do not greet
the Jews and the Christians before they greet you and when
you meet any one of them on the roads force him to go to
the narrowest part of it.[67]

The antipathy for Christians is reinforced by the fact that
faithful Muslims who pray five times daily will, in the
course of their prayers, repeat seventeen times a day in
Arabic the first sura of the Qur'an, known as the *fatiha*,
which is regarded as the most important sura in the whole
Qur'an. The sixth and seventh verses of the *fatiha* run:

Guide us to the Straight Way. The Way of those on whom
You have bestowed Your Grace, not (the way) of those who
earned Your Anger (such as the Jews), nor of those who
went astray (such as the Christians).

Although the Arabic does not contain the words in
brackets, these are added to the English translation to
show Muslims how they should interpret this text according
to the guidance of the *hadith*, i.e. they are supposed to
think of Jews as those who have earned God's anger and
Christians as those who have gone astray. Such a message,
repeated seventeen times a day, does not make for easy
friendships with non-Muslims.

Kafirun

Those outside the *umma* tend to be despised and rejected
as thoroughly as those inside the *umma* are embraced. A
non-Muslim is a *kafir* (plural *kafirun* or *kuffar*). It is hard
to convey in English the gross insult conveyed by this
technical term. Translating it as "infidel" conveys something
of the nuance of "enemy" but still lacks the abusive quality.

The habitual use by many Muslims in conversation
with each other of the word *kafir* for "non-Muslim" serves
to reinforce an attitude of contempt towards non-Muslims.
Even though Sir Iqbal Sacranie, secretary-general of the

---

67   Sahih Muslim Hadith Book 26, Number 5389, narrated by Abu Harayrah

Muslim Council of Britain, has told British Muslims not to use this term, it is for many normal usage. Dr Taj Hargey has said that it is heard

"ad infinitum and ad nauseam. It's there. It's with us. We see it from the time you're a child, you're given this idea that those people they are *kafir*, they're unbelievers. They are not equal to you. They are different from you. You are superior to them because you have the truth, they don't have the truth ... So we have this from a very young age."[68]

The barrier caused by the use of the word "*kafir*" might be compared with the greater barrier to friendship with Pakistanis for white Britons who normally call them "Pakis" compared with white Britons who normally use more respectful vocabulary.

Gifts and hospitality
Hospitality and the exchange of gifts are two of the linchpins of relationships in the East (and have importance in the West as well). But what happens when Christians try to do this with Muslims? Often they will find that they are warmly welcomed into the Muslim home and plied with delicious food, but cannot persuade the Muslims to make a return visit to the Christian home. If conservative Muslims do come to visit the Christians, they may refuse any form of refreshment. This is more than just concern about eating non-*halal* food as there are plenty of Islamically acceptable kinds of food which can be offered. Two factors are the cultural concept of Christians as religiously "unclean" (arising from the discriminatory laws against them in the *shari'a*) and the fact that accepting a meal means owing a favour to the host. In addition, there are *hadiths* recording Muhammad's disapproval of pictures, which are commonly found in Western homes. For example:

---

68   Interviewed by John Ware in "A Question of Leadership", Panorama, BBC 1 (21 August 2005).

> Abu Talha, a companion of Allah's Apostle and one of those who fought at the Badr together with Allah's Apostle told me that Allah's Apostle said, "Angels do not enter a house in which there is a dog or a picture." He meant the images of creatures that have souls.[69]

As Muslims in the West become more religiously observant, they are growing less willing to enter Christian homes. Furthermore, since dogs are considered "unclean", as suggested in the *hadith* above, and contact with a dog would make a Muslim unclean, many Muslims will try to avoid entering a home where there is a dog.

With regard to gifts, Muslims will often be generous givers but reluctant to receive. The local imam may bestow a beautiful copy of the Qur'an on the local minister but brush aside the Bible which he is offered in return. This was the experience of the Bishop of Hildesheim, Germany, who was warmly welcomed to the mosque by the imam. The imam presented the grateful bishop with a Qur'an but rejected with horror the Bible which the bishop tried to present to him in return.[70] Muslims are always on the alert for opportunities for mission, such as giving Qur'ans to non-Muslims. But they guard themselves against anything that might serve to deflect them from the way of Islam, such as the scriptures of another faith. Many Muslims feel they would be sinning if they even touched a copy of the Bible. A book of instructions for new converts to Islam tells them the attitude they should have to the Bible:

> The previously divinely revealed books have suffered a great deal of distortion, additions and deletions, as Allah has mentioned in the Qur'an. Therefore it is not allowed for Muslims to read or look at them. The exception is if the

---

69   Sahih Al-Bukhari Hadith 5.338, narrated by Ibn Abbas
70   Bassam Tibi, "Blessed are those who are Lied to: Christian–Islamic Dialogue is Based on Deceit – and furthers Western Wishful Thinking", in *Die Zeit* (29 May 2002). Professor Tibi is a Muslim of Syrian origin, now at Goettingen University, Germany.

person is well-grounded in knowledge and desires to show what has occurred in them of distortions and contradictions.[71]

On the other hand, Muslims who are seeking a spiritual reality and have not found it in Islam may be immensely grateful to receive a Bible or a DVD of the Jesus film. Christians should not refrain from offering such materials, which are often the means by which Muslims become Christians, but should understand the possibility of their gift being rejected.

Places of worship

Exchange visits between the church and the mosque might seem to some a good way to foster Christian-Muslim relations. Even better, it might seem, would be inviting Muslims to share in the leading of Christian worship or Christian celebrations. Muslim leaders will probably be much happier to accept a Christian invitation to the church than an invitation to a private home. Sometimes the initial suggestion of the visit to the church may even come from the Muslims. Typically the pattern is that the imam preaches in the church and the minister merely prays in the mosque. This is seen by the Muslims as a victory for them. As in the attempted exchange of scriptures, the Muslims will use every opportunity to promote their faith and to prevent the similar promotion of Christianity.

It is striking how one-sided these "exchanges" often are. It seems that Christians are expected to do all the learning and Muslims all the teaching. Christians involved in any such initiatives should strive to ensure there is a level playing field with both Christians and Muslims able to share their faith as well as to listen to what the others have to say.

It is mystifying why some church leaders seem to

---

71   *Answers to Common Questions from New Muslims,* collected by Abu Anas Ali ibn Husain Abu Lauz, translated by Jamaal al-Din M. Zarabozo (Ann Arbor, Michigan: Islamic Assembly of North America, 1995) p.27

endorse an asymmetrical kind of relationship by inviting
Muslims to share their faith from a church pulpit without
ensuring that there is a reciprocal opportunity for
Christians to share their faith with Muslims. David Gillett,
Anglican Bishop of Bolton and co-chair of the Christian-
Muslim Forum in England, suggests five ways to develop
relationships with Muslims in the UK, starting with
"How many of us have invited a Muslim to speak to our
congregation about their faith?"[72] Many Christians would
want to plead with Bishop Gillett not to promote
Christian-Muslim relations by having Islam preached to
Christians, given that Islam not only contradicts the
Christian faith but furthermore calls for the killing of any
Muslim who becomes a Christian. They would ask him to
find a more neutral and balanced way of developing good
relationships without such a one-sided dominance of one
faith over the other. Ultimately, biblical truth must take
precedence over both political pragmatism and good
community race and interfaith relations. Those who do
not discern this may find themselves unwittingly on the road
towards apostasy.

Muslim leadership in Christian events is a very different matter from inviting Muslim individuals to be part
of the congregation at Christian worship. Stephen Lowe,
Bishop of Hulme, urges Christians in Manchester, UK, to
invite Muslims to tell Christians about their faith, to organ-
ise joint Christian/Muslim school assemblies, and to replace
an annual "June Whit Walk" (a celebration of the Christian Whitsun) every other year with a joint Christian-
Muslim "Walk of Faiths".

> One of the best days of the year for me was the June Whit
> Walks where it was a privilege for me to walk alongside the

---

72   David Gillett, "Banda Aceh – Symbol of our Inter Faith Agenda" in *The Reader* Vol. 102,
No. 4 (Winter 2005) p. 8

Muslim Lord Mayor of Manchester and the Mayor of Salford on what is at heart a Christian celebration. **Why not every other year make this into a Walk of Faiths with us celebrating together through the streets of Manchester what we share rather than what divides us? What a witness to the city and Greater Manchester about our unity in a divided and broken world.**[73]

Few Muslim leaders would dream of compromising their faith for the sake of the feelings of Christians or to show inter-religious solidarity, so it is hard to understand why Bishop Lowe wants to turn opportunities for Christian witness into opportunities to promote the Islamic faith, effectively neutralising the Christian message. Furthermore, the "editing" of the Christian faith could well be interpreted by Muslims as acceptance of the superiority of Islam.

A situation that sometimes arises is that a request is made by Muslims who have no mosque building of their own to use the church premises for their Friday prayers. It may seem the act of a good neighbour to say yes, especially if the church is not used at Friday lunchtimes. But the issue of the Muslim attitude to territory (see pages 20-21, 69-70) must be considered, as well as the reality of the spiritual dimension and in particular the possibility of cursing prayers (see pages 37-40). Even when curses are not being prayed, the normal Islamic creed, which is recited whenever Muslims pray, specifically denies the truth of the Christian Gospel with its words "There is no god but God, and Muhammad is the apostle of God". (See pages 50-51.) Should a church building be the scene of such anti-Christian affirmations? Another factor to take into account is the message which this dual use of the church sends to the local community that

---

73   Stephen Lowe, "In a Divided World, the Best Answer is to Unite" in Manchester Diocese's magazine *Crux* (August 2005), p.7. Emphasis in original.

"Islam and Christianity are one and the same".

In the light of this it is probably best not to use either church buildings or mosques for Christian-Muslim encounters, but to use a neutral venue.

New mosques

Another difficult issue for Christians comes when Muslims seek to build a mosque in their local area. In a liberal Western democracy this might seem at first glance to be a non-issue – surely it is only fair to allow them their own place of worship, indeed to facilitate their application for planning permission? By the same reasoning, Christians might feel that it would be showing the love of Christ to assist Muslims in their mosque-building project, for example, by raising funds. But there are implications which should be weighed carefully.

Firstly, there is the familiar issue of religious territoriality, not only the ideology and spirituality but also the practicality. A mosque building consolidates and strengthens the Muslim community, both psychologically and physically. It simultaneously weakens any outreach efforts that churches may have been making in the area to, say, Muslim youngsters through church youth clubs. Questions should be asked about whether the size of the building is proportional to the number of Muslims in the area. Another question is the size of the building compared with the nearest church (which may turn out to be surprisingly near). Muslims often make a point of building a mosque close to a church and taller than the church – an illustration in bricks and mortar of their superiority. Christians may feel that it is unchristian to compete for visible status in this way, but they should at least be aware of how local Muslims will be thinking, both now and in the future. Another important point concerns the theological persuasion of the mosque – will it encourage radicalism? Finally, on the issue of fairness and justice, it is valid to lift one's gaze from the local community and pan around to consider places of worship worldwide. There are many Muslim-majority contexts where Christians find it difficult to get permission for sufficient church buildings. This happens in countries which are popular holiday destinations for Westerners, for example, Malaysia and Egypt. In Saudi Arabia no church buildings are allowed at all. Could there be an argument for trying somehow to negotiate for reciprocal permission for Christian minorities in Muslim contexts before allowing Muslim minorities in the West to build as many mosques as they want?

Rt Rev. James Jones, Anglican Bishop of Liverpool, UK, and an evangelical, has accepted an invitation to be a patron of a local mosque on the basis of his personal friendship with the imam and that the building was a historic building. While delighted at his friendship with the imam, the question arises as to how he can lend his name to support a place of worship for a faith which contradicts the message of the Bible. It is doubtful whether he would accept an invitation to be the patron of any other non-Christian place of worship, such as a Mormon temple, and therefore difficult to understand why he makes an exception for Islam.

Joining in Islamic worship
Sometimes Christians seek to develop good relations with Muslims by sharing in Islamic spiritual disciplines. These well-meant and often sacrificial gestures must be considered with great caution. For example, some Christians fast alongside Muslims during Ramadan. But what does this mean in the spiritual realm? The spiritual highlight of Ramadan is the "Night of Power" which marks the date on which Muhammad received the first revelation of the Qur'an.[74] Can a Christian really be involved in celebrating

---

74   Many Muslims consider 27th Ramadan to be the Night of Power but certain groups take other dates in Ramadan.

something which so profoundly contradicts the Gospel?

Some Christians join in with Muslim prayers, for example, when breaking daily the Ramadan fast or when starting the fast again each morning. While there is no problem with a Christian praying the simple prayer before breaking the fast, it is very different situation if a Christian joins in the prayers before starting the fast. These prayers involve reciting both the creed and the *fatiha*, and a Christian saying these words would effectively be denying their faith.

Christian-Muslim relations should be free of "Christian sentimentality" and of a *dhimmi*-like spirit of submission and appeasement on the part of the Christians. Blurring the boundaries does not help the relationship. As between neighbours in a street, clear boundaries lead to better relationships.

"Dialogue"

One frequently hears of interfaith "dialogue" initiatives between Christian leaders and Muslim leaders, by which is usually meant debate and discussion, perhaps on a particular area of mutual concern. This approach has some inherent risks, the first of which is the ambiguity of the term "dialogue".[75] The New Testament term *dialegomai*, as used of Paul (Acts 17:17) means argument with a view of convincing the listener. For Paul, dialogue was a form of evangelism. Paul did not gather the pagan religious leaders together for a round table discussion on religious commonalities and for mutual enrichment. Rather he argued with them to try to convince them (Acts 17:22-31). Paul had a burning desire to lead people to an encounter with the crucified and risen Lord.

However, most Christians involved in dialogue have no intention of persuading the Muslims with whom they are speaking to become Christians, wishing only to find

---

75   There are many varieties of dialogue including human, discursive and existential.

areas of common ground on which all can agree. They approach such meetings simply as conversations, rather than as dialogue in the New Testament sense. There are only a small number of Christians who use dialogue as a starting-point for evangelism. It might be better, therefore, to describe such encounters more accurately and neutrally, perhaps as "discussion meetings".

On the other hand, Muslims will normally seize any opportunity to advance the cause of Islam, and that would include using dialogue initiatives to try to convert Christians. Ironically the Muslims' understanding of "dialogue" is much more in line with Paul's than is that of most Christians. Muslims find it hard to believe that Christians are **not** seeking to convert them during the dialogue process; they cannot understand why Christians would not make use of this convenient opportunity for evangelism. As a result Muslims often suspect that such dialogue is a form of Christian deception.

Some of the other risks involved in such encounters are:

1. There is a likelihood that Christians will do all the giving and Muslims all the taking. This is inherent in the different nature of the two religions. As has already been seen, Christianity stresses meekness, humility, confession, repentance, sacrifice and self-denial. Islam prizes power, domination and honour. Muslims will usually present their case as victims, make accusations against Christianity and demand compensatory actions. At the same time they will fiercely resist any discussion of Muslim faults such as the bloody history of *jihad* (which they will usually deny) and the discriminatory treatment of Christians in Muslim contexts.

2. Key vocabulary is understood differently by Muslims and Christians, so there is a great risk of misunderstanding and of talking at cross purposes. For example,

the word "peace" for Muslims carries the connotation of establishing peace and order by spreading Islamic rule and authority across the globe.[76] Similarly, when Muslims claim that Islamic societies were historically tolerant of non-Muslims, they mean that the non-Muslims were not killed, expelled or forcibly converted. This is very different from the modern Western understanding of tolerance as implying full equality of status and rights. Other words which can carry different meanings and connotations are "equality" itself, "self-defence", "terrorism", "innocent", "fasting" and "Holy Spirit" to name but a few.

3. Some Muslims consider any interaction with Christians as a justification for the use of *taqiyya* [dissimulation] in the cause of Islam. As has been seen, some also hold that it is permissible for Muslims to break agreements made with non-Muslims. So any undertakings or pledges made by the Muslim side cannot necessarily be relied on, nor can any factual information given be automatically accepted as true.

Bearing in mind all these factors, it is very difficult to ensure that formal Christian-Muslim discussions do not become simply a search for the lowest common denominator, in which much that is essential to each religion is downplayed or – more often – completely ignored. Discussion of this kind – which is lacking to a greater or lesser degree in honesty, integrity, transparency or truth – may promote short-term peace of a kind. But unless it tackles the real issues of society and seeks with honesty and openness to develop methods of living together and addressing the treatment of minorities on both sides, the process will

---

76   Ismail Raji al-Faruqi, *Islam and Other Faiths* (Leicester: The Islamic Foundation, 1998) p. 91: "Evidently, far from being a national state, the Islamic State is a world order in which numerous religious communities, national or transnational, co-exist in peace. It is a universal *Pax Islamica* ... Its constitution is divine law, valid for all ..."

ultimately be futile.

The outrageous injustices suffered by Christian minorities in the Muslim world must not be forgotten by Western Christians involved in discussion with Muslims in the West. If they are not raised in discussion, then those minorities will have been betrayed by their Christian brothers and sisters in the West; they will have been sacrificed for the sake of peace on Western streets.

It is adding insult to injury when Western Christians "dialogue" with Muslim authorities in Muslim countries without involving the national Christians. Christians in the West should help and strengthen the national Churches in Muslim countries, who are in an extremely vulnerable position. Western Churches should take care to avoid finding themselves in a position where they are dialoguing with the Muslims and have bypassed the national Church. This is to treat the national Christians as if they were children, lacking the wisdom or ability to speak to their Muslim compatriots.

Furthermore, a test of "genuine" encounter would be whether both Christian and Muslim partners are willing to accept converts speaking on the other side. All too often, Muslims involved in dialogue will include white converts to Islam but Christians from a Muslim background will not be allowed to participate on behalf of Christians.

Christian-Muslim cooperation on non-religious projects
It is sometimes argued that it is good for Christians and Muslims to seek areas of common concern where they can work together. Such areas would include protecting the traditional family, anti-abortion issues, ecology, and relief of poverty. The logic behind this suggestion is that both Christians and Muslims share a common society and must seek to advance the common good. In such

common ventures, there can be a lack of understanding on the Christians' part regarding possible Muslim aims; it is important that the Christians should first gain a realistic knowledge of the nature of Islam, its agenda and how Muslims view their relationship with Christians. Traditionally there have been two viewpoints about Christians working with other groups to achieve social change. The first is to avoid working with non-Christians and simply to trust God and believe that he will work through Christian believers. The second is to work with like-minded people who are motivated by Christian principles whether or not they are committed Christians. A good example of the second is Wilberforce and the abolition of the slave trade.

Today, however, the second position is being broadened to include those of other faiths, particularly Muslims. The question arises as to why the limit should be drawn at adherents of world faiths. Why not include Mormons and Jehovah's Witnesses, or people of goodwill who are humanists and atheists? These would be just as capable of engaging in good works motivated by good values. Careful thought should be given to defining the boundaries of those we can work with. Great confusion can be caused by emphasising faith groups as if they have values in common not shared by people without faith, or as if all faiths share the same values as the Christian faith. This sends a message that all faiths are fundamentally the same. Where it is needful to engage in common causes – and this is becoming increasingly necessary in today's world – should not our aim be to work with people of goodwill (whether they have a faith or not) rather than specifically with people of faith e.g. Muslims? It is hard to find any warrant in the Bible for interfaith cooperation. In fact it can be argued that cooperation with other faiths actually led to the decline of Israel and brought judgement upon the people of God.

Christian-Muslim cooperation on overseas aid, relief and development

Natural disasters such as famines, earthquakes and tsunamis afflict entire populations, regardless of their faith. Relieving needs in such situations might seem an ideal way for Christians to show their love by cooperating with and funding Muslim-run initiatives. However, it must be recalled that when Muslims give their *zakat* offerings these are to be used for the benefit of their fellow-Muslims (see page 19). In accordance with this theology, Muslim aid agencies do not usually help all disaster victims irrespective of faith. The norm is that Muslim agencies only help Muslims. After the tsunami of 26th December 2004, many Christians in the strongly Islamic Indonesian province of Aceh found that they were refused aid unless they agreed to convert to Islam. This is by no means unusual.

It can be very hard for Christians to grasp this mindset, which is so deeply embedded in the Muslim psyche that it is often not verbalised, but simply taken for granted. In Islam there is simply no concept of loving outside the *umma* or of loving one's enemy. (Equally, it can be very hard for Muslims to understand that Christians may delight in giving aid to those of other faiths, with no strings attached – a policy which therefore often raises Muslim suspicions.) It is also important to realise that even though a Muslim aid agency may say on its website that it helps people of all faiths, this is highly unlikely to be what really happens on the ground. Certainly, Christian minorities in Muslim-majority contexts do not expect to receive help from Islamic sources. Even government aid might be denied them if local officials in charge of distribution decide not to give it to Christian villages or Christian families.

Another factor which applies to some Muslim aid agencies is the close link in the Muslim mind between helping Muslim needy and supporting the general Muslim cause. This means that donations made for "the poor" could possibly end up being used to fund *da'wa* or even *jihad*.

If Christians choose to make donations to Muslim aid agencies or to become associated with Muslim aid agencies, they must be aware that they are endorsing at the very least discrimination against their Christian brothers and sisters, and possibly activities which are far more anti-Christian than that. When Christian Aid donated £250,000 to Islamic Relief to assist the victims of the Pakistan earthquake of October 2005, did they consider that those who had specifically chosen a Christian agency through which to make their donation might not have wanted their gifts to be channelled through a Muslim agency?

When a senior evangelical bishop in the Church of England visited Afghanistan with an Islamic aid agency, what message did that send in a country where Christians are severely persecuted and converts from Islam have been killed? When another bishop in the Church of England visited Aceh, Indonesia, with Muslim Aid in July 2005 and cut the ribbon at the opening ceremony of the first new house for tsunami victims to be completed with funds from Muslim Aid, what message did that send to the beleaguered Acehnese Christians? Many Muslim Acehnese had already made it clear that they wanted to take advantage of the post-tsunami chaos to cleanse their province of Christians. The English bishop, who has a leading role in Christian-Muslim relations in the UK, was aware that there were non-Muslims in Aceh affected by the tsunami but apparently he made no effort to meet them, assist them, or affirm them in any way.[77] It is understandable that he was thrilled with the "immense privilege" of speaking at the opening ceremony of the Muslim Aid house, and "deeply moved" to be invited to cut the ribbon "hand in hand with a Muslim friend". But it is very hard to comprehend his attitude if indeed he did not show any concern for the welfare of his Christian brothers and sisters in Indonesia, nor take time to find out how they were faring.

It is interesting to note that the group of British Muslims and Christians visiting Aceh to look at relief work after the tsunami was sponsored by the UK's Foreign Office. This raises the question of how much Western governments may be involved in driving forward the interfaith agenda.

Christian-Muslim cooperation on religious projects
In these days of rampant secularism, some Christians are beginning to feel that they have a bond with people of any faith, as religious believers stand together against atheism, materialism, immorality and other features of secular society. This is possibly why some Western Christians have been willing to entertain suggestions such as that made by an imam in Woking, UK that a 2007 calendar be produced with texts from both the Bible and the Qur'an to be given to all Muslims and Christians in Woking. The local Christian cross-cultural ministry, whose aim is to "reach the nations in Woking", thought this might be "a great way to spread the Word". One wonders if they had considered the implications. Would the calendar, for example, put sura 4, verse 171, (which denies the Sonship of Christ) next to John 3:16, as if "balancing out" the truth claims? How far should Christians be involved in

---

77   This is inferred from the fact that the bishop does not mention anything about Christians in Aceh in an article he wrote describing his visit. David Gillett, "Banda Aceh – Symbol of our Inter Faith Agenda" in *The Reader* Vol. 102, No. 4 (Winter 2005) pp.7-8

promoting the Qur'an, a book which denies Christ's death and resurrection (see page 51). Such a project could run the severe risk of sending the message to Christians that the Bible and Qur'an are equally valid as the Word of God.

Reconciliation

Many current Christian initiatives towards Muslims describe their aim as "reconciliation" though it is unclear what the biblical justification for this choice of terminology is. Space does not permit a detailed study of the concept of reconciliation in the Bible, but the key passage often quoted in the context of Christian-Muslim relations, that is, the "ministry of reconciliation" (2 Corinthians 5:18-20), is clearly defined as reconciliation between sinful humans and God, not reconciliation between people of different faiths. Similarly most of the other New Testament references to reconciliation are defined within the text as reconciliation to God (Romans 5:10; 11:15; Ephesians 2:16; Colossians 1:20,22). The only exceptions are reconciliation between estranged spouses (1 Corinthians 7:11) and between fellow believers who have quarrelled (Matthew 5:24). As for the Old Testament, the whole tenor is against any kind of rapprochement between the people of God and followers of another faith. The word reconciliation is used in some translations in the context of atonement for sin i.e. reconciliation of sinners with God. The one exception occurs in 1 Samuel 29:4 where the Philistines anticipate that David may seek to be reconciled to Saul and thus turn traitor to them.

While we are called to love all human beings regardless of creed, race or culture, there is no call in the Bible for Christians as a body to seek reconciliation with other faiths. (Rather, such action would stand in danger of judgement, at least according to the Old Testament.) This is not to deny the need for Christians and Muslims to find ways of addressing the causes of contemporary conflict with a view to sharing the globe harmoniously. In this area of conflict it is vital for Christians to be peacemakers (Matthew 5:9). But peace should never be made at the expense of theological distinctives or at the expense of righteousness, justice and truth.

Hans Kung has argued "No peace among the nations without peace between the religions". The difficulty with this argument is that it presupposes a level playing field. Whereas Christianity (bar some aspects of Orthodox denominations) has abandoned religious territoriality, Islam has not. Therefore to argue for peace without a sea-change in Islamic understanding of territory is not viable.

There are also Christians who propound the need for reconciliation in the context of specific perceived historical injustices perpetrated by Christians on Muslims e.g. the Crusades and colonialism. The methodology is usually to apologise for what European Christians are deemed to have done. The motivation is usually either to prepare the way for the effective evangelisation of Muslims by seeking their forgiveness or simply to facilitate harmonious Christian-Muslim relations. Some also believe that such apologies will cleanse the land where blood has been spilled and so usher in God's blessings. Sadly such positions are based on weak theology and inaccurate historical understanding. This is not to suggest that Christians have never failed and that there are never times when apology is appropriate. But apologising for the Crusades and for colonialism sends inappropriate cultural signals and can do more harm than good in that they reinforce the Muslims' sense of grievance against Christians. The tragic result is often a backlash of Muslim violence against vulnerable Christian minorities in the Muslim countries. Reconciliation has no value if it is devoid of righteousness, justice and truth.

There is no theology of reconciliation in the *shari'a*, only a theology of temporary treaties. Permanent peace can only exist within *Dar al-Islam*, i.e. where Muslims are in control. A further complication is that reconciliation is one of the situations in which Muslims are specifically permitted to lie, according to the doctrine of *taqiyya* (see page 34.).

Mission

Christian spirituality cannot remove mission from its core. As has been said, the Church is mission, and a mission-less Church is a Christ-less Church. The Church's encounter with Islam must carry a missionary dimension. This dimension will involve a loving, compassionate service that proclaims the truths of the Gospel so that the Holy Spirit may bring conversion. With this will come the Christian call for justice for those who choose to follow Christ.

Mission to Muslims will be rooted in prayer and intercession and will challenge the spiritual principalities and powers that make up Islam. It will deal with power encounters as did the Lord Jesus in his ministry.

None of the above cautions about Christian-Muslim relations should prevent Christians from seeking to make friends with Muslims, to show them love and compassion, to share their faith with Muslims, or to invite them to church as a member of the congregation (as opposed to inviting Muslims to preach or lead prayer or worship in a church service).

As there are many works devoted to advising Christians on the practicalities of sharing their faith with Muslims, this subject will not be covered here.[78] Much help can also be found by drawing on the experience of missionaries

---

78   A particularly good one is Malcolm Steer, *A Christian's Evangelistic Pocket Guide to Islam* (Fearn, Tain, UK: Christian Focus Publications, 2003)

working amongst Muslims in the Muslim world and in the West, and also on the expertise of Christians from the Muslim world living in the West.

Convert care
This important subject should perhaps not come under the heading of Christian-Muslim relations because it is really Christian-Christian relations. However, it is placed here to emphasise that it should be an integral part of mission to Muslims.

Compared with new believers from a secular or nominally Christian background, the needs of converts from Islam are usually far greater. This is true of practical, emotional and spiritual needs. The challenge to churches is to care for the converts and meet these needs. Many Muslim converts who have not been cared for well enough eventually choose to return to Islam, a faith which excels at caring for its own.

Apostasy law in Islam
Conversion from Islam is viewed as treachery against the Muslim community and this is the basis for the extreme reaction of Muslim friends, family, colleagues etc. Indeed, according to Islamic law, adult male apostates from Islam should be executed as if they were traitors. While the death sentence for apostasy is only part of the law of the land in a handful of countries (e.g. Saudi Arabia, Iran, Sudan, Qatar, Mauritania) it is generally acknowledged by the vast majority of Muslims to be part of their theology. Hence the persecution of converts from Islam by a multiplicity of methods of attacking the person, their property, relationships and freedoms. This can even include murder, to which some Muslim police officers would turn a blind eye.

A British imam seeking to promote interfaith relations

has proposed a scheme whereby Muslims may be permitted to convert to certain Christian denominations (i.e. not be persecuted for doing so). He proposes that agreements could be made between Muslim authorities and the Orthodox and Roman Catholic churches. The denominational leaders would have to pledge their solidarity with various inter-national Muslim causes (Palestine, Iraq etc.) and condemn US foreign policy. On these conditions, the Muslims would agree not to persecute any Muslims who converted to these particular denominations. The imam envisages that Anglicans – being such a broad church – would most likely have to be dealt with in two groups. He anticipates that it would probably be possible to make an agreement with Anglo-Catholics but not with evangelical Anglicans. He doubts that converts to other Protestant denominations would be eligible for such agreements. (Separately he requires restrictions on foreign missionaries evangelising in Muslim countries.)

Such an initiative should not be countenanced by Christians, as it makes the Church submit to the requirements of Islam and effectively enshrines the continued persecution of converts to conservative evangelical Christianity, divides the Church, and forces Christians to abandon the Great Commission without making any such requirement for Muslims to stop engaging in *da'wa*. This is contrary to Article 18 of the United Nations Universal Declaration of Human Rights which guarantees the freedom to change one's religion or belief.

What converts suffer
The "crime" of apostasy brings enormous shame on the relatives of the convert, and therefore the relatives will go to any lengths to try to persuade the convert to return to Islam and thus restore the family's honour. Often baptism is the point at which severe persecution begins.

A typical reaction will be threats and perhaps violence from some family members, or emotional blackmail such as a distraught mother saying she will kill herself if her beloved child does not return to Islam. Bearing in mind that the closest bond in many Muslim families is between mother and son, this can be extremely hard for a young man to bear. Another kind of threat or pressure is financial, for example, refusing to assist a convert student with their fees or support. A married convert may find that the spouse leaves, taking the children too. Many converts have to leave home – either they are thrown out or they have to escape the pressure and violence. There can also be rejection and violence from the wider Muslim community, for example, stoning, arson, beatings – all these have been experienced by converts from Islam living in the UK.

So the local church **must** become the convert's new family. Their "family responsibilities" must be as wide-ranging and deep in commitment as a Muslim family's are (Muslim families tend to be more supportive than a typical white British family). That includes providing accommodation, friendship, fellowship and financial support if necessary. The emotional pain of rejection by family and friends is something which cannot quickly be healed, but the continued patient love of Christians plays an essential part.

In Muslim countries it can be very risky for Christians who care for converts from Islam and sadly some churches will therefore not get involved. But in the West there is nothing to stop churches taking responsibility for caring for such converts. The fact that some British church leaders have publicly refused to accept Muslim converts amounts to disobedience to Jesus' command to his disciples to love one another. The motive appears to be a fear of jeopardising harmonious Christian-Muslim relations locally.

Relations between Christians and the Muslim community are important, but the needs of converts from Islam – Christians who are carrying a heavy cross – must take precedence. It is grotesque and nonsensical to neglect the needs of Christian converts from Islam for the sake for friendship with Muslims; we must not sacrifice the members of our own family on the altar of our post-modern relativism.

New Christians from a Muslim background often feel in great need of spiritual guidance. They have left a faith which is characterised by a multitude of rules governing even which foot to step over a threshold with, how to lie in bed, and how to relieve oneself.[79] Their new faith does not have this framework of rules, so converts can feel unsure how to behave in many situations. They need discipleship training to help them learn to live and grow as Christians.

Asylum-seekers
Many British churches may have links with Muslim converts who are not British citizens and do not have "indefinite leave to remain" in the UK. Such individuals could be sent back to their country of origin, which in turn could endanger their lives because of Islam's apostasy laws and the effect this has on Muslim society. The same situation can arise in other Western countries but appears to be particularly acute in the UK, where many immigration officers do not yet seem to understand or believe the real dangers which converts face. They often fail to distinguish between Christian-background Christians and Muslim-background Christians, and do not recognise that the former may be safe while the latter are at risk. They also often seem to be unaware that what the law or constitution of the country says about guaranteeing

---

79   See, for example, Marwan Ibrahim Al-Kaysi, *Morals and Manners in Islam: A Guide to Islamic Adab* (Leicester: The Islamic Foundation, 1996)

freedom of religion may be contradicted by what happens in practice on the ground.

Converts who do not have a good command of English face the additional risk of possibly having a Muslim interpreter who may not do justice to what they are saying, or who may report them to the local Muslim community, thus placing them in further danger.

Churches must exert themselves to assist such individuals or families in their legal battles. Finding a lawyer experienced in such cases is vital. Barnabas Fund is happy to provide documents affirming the dangers which converts from Islam face.[80]

Justice

Christians in the West have the freedom to speak out and lobby on any issue they like. There is therefore a challenge for the Church in terms of making use of this freedom to be a voice for persecuted Christians in Muslim contexts who cannot speak for themselves. The Bible teaches clearly that God loves justice, and Western Christians are in a position to work for justice for their fellow-Christians who suffer discrimination and oppression for no other reason than their Christian faith.

Key issues are the apostasy law and *dhimmi* status as enshrined in the *shari'a*, which includes discrimination against Christians in terms of legal testimony and compensation. (See pages 67-68.) The theology of *jihad* lies behind some anti-Christian violence, such as that which various provinces of Indonesia have seen in the early years of the twenty-first century. Another important issue is that of "blasphemy" against Muhammad, who is so venerated in Pakistan that there is a mandatory death

---

80   Contact Barnabas Fund, the Old Rectory, River Street, Pewsey, Wiltshire SN9 5DB, UK, phone 08700 603 900, fax 08700 603 901, from outside UK phone +44 1672 564938, fax +44 1672 565030, e-mail info@barnabasfund.org

sentence for "defiling" his name. As has already been noted, Christians are particularly vulnerable to malicious accusations under this law, because of the tendency of some Muslim judges to believe the word of a Muslim over that of a Christian (in accordance with *shari'a*).

Another kind of injustice faced repeatedly by Christian minorities in the Muslim world is the way in which they are made scapegoats for the actions of governments and others in "Christian" countries of the West. Thus in January and February 2006 Christians in Iraq, Nigeria, Turkey and Pakistan and many other countries faced threats or actual violence in response to the publication in a number of secular newspapers in Europe of caricatures of Muham-mad which had originally been drawn by Danish cartoonists in 2005. Even Christian children were victim-ised for the actions of the European journalists when church schools in Pakistan were attacked. As the Bishop of Peshawar said, "We [Pakistani Christians] have not done anything; the cartoons are nothing to do with us. They [the Muslim rioters] do not comprehend or accept that Pakistani Christ-ians are not Westerners."

Furthermore, Christian minorities have to accept the desecration of what is sacred to them without being able to complain. The Pakistani rioters at Mardan on 6th February 2006 were reported to have made a large cross, then trampled on it and burned it. They were retaliating for what they held to be an insult to their prophet (as were hundreds of thousands of other Muslims around the world) in the full knowledge that the Christian minority in Pakistan could do nothing about it.

It is possible that the freedom to protest against such injustice may not continue in the West indefinitely. Victoria State, Australia, already has its Racial and Religious Tolerance Act (2001), which has been used to prevent

Christians from teaching other Christians about Islam. The UK narrowly escaped similar legislation being passed in January 2006, which could well have stopped any criticism of Islam or its treatment of non-Muslim minorities. Christians must take up this challenge while they still can.

The issue of justice for Christian minorities is one which – like the issue of converts from Islam – can easily become sidelined in the desire for "dialogue" and good Christian-Muslim relations. But this amounts to a betrayal of vulnerable Christians. In January 2006 Dr Mouneer Hanna Anis, the Anglican Bishop in Egypt, met with senior Egyptian Muslim clerics at Trinity College, Dublin to launch a resource pack called "The Hand of History (Exploring Christian/Muslim Dialogue)". One of the Muslims was the Grand Mufti of Egypt and Rector of the prestigious Al-Azhar University in Cairo, the leading institution of Sunni Islam worldwide. The other Muslim was Al-Azhar's president of the Dialogue with Monotheistic Religions.

The bishop made several statements about the situation of Egyptian Christians to the effect that those of Christian background had virtually no problems and even converts from Islam had only minor difficulties. Such statements cannot be described as anything less than extremely misleading (not to say painful to those whose sufferings were being denied), and dialoguing in rose-tinted spectacles seems at best pointless. One wonders whether the bishop realised how his statements could be quoted by others to the detriment of the very needy and vulnerable Christians of Egypt. The Metropolitan of Glastonbury, who heads the British Orthodox Church which is an integral part of the Coptic Orthodox Church, wrote to the Archbishop of Canterbury, criticising Dr Mouneer's assertions, pointing out the grave difficulties facing

Egyptian Christians, and finishing:

> Brotherly support from the Anglican community world-
> wide, and especially in Egypt is something much to be
> valued, but if it is to be of lasting value in enabling the diverse
> religious communities to live together in harmony, it is also
> necessary to highlight the source and reality of the problems
> which militate against this. [81]

---

81   Letter from Metropolitan Seraphim of the British Orthodox Church to Dr Rowan
      Williams, Archbishop of Canterbury (6 February 2006)

CONCLUSION

This book has sought to demonstrate that Islam is an all-encompassing entity which includes not only the inner life but also, and especially, the outer life of an individual's role in family, community and society. Neither law nor politics nor military service lies outside of Islam. It has also sought to show the rigid, highly specified and unchanging nature of Islam which leaves little or no freedom for the individual's conscience or personality to be expressed, or for Islam itself to alter or adapt. That the contemporary Islamic renewal movement is seeking to impose the age-old Islamic societal norms wherever it can, even by force, should be no surprise as it is the very essence of Islam to take control of earthly structures.

The crisis which arose in early 2006 over the publication of cartoons of Muhammad the Islamic prophet well illustrated the way in which Islam operates. Islam has the capacity for thinking strategically, acting structurally and working towards submission of non-Muslims. This is done primarily through fear. The West is now at a crossroads in its relationship with Islam. Threats and intimidation have resulted in pusillanimous governments, compliant media and an insipid Church. The fear which is beginning to shape government and media has now sadly entered into the Church, with Christians increasingly unwilling or unable to critique Islam. Either they embrace dialogue and interfaith relations and acquiesce to Muslim demands on the Muslims' terms or they retreat into a ghetto-like mentality borne of fear. For the Christian we are told that perfect love casts out fear, for there can be no fear in love (1 John 4:18). Christians who truly love God and their Saviour, the Lord Jesus Christ, will not fear what either people or ideology or false religion can do to them. The time has come for the Church to stand up and be bold in the face of an oncoming darkness. The Church needs great faith and courage to be strong in our day. She can do so with the conviction and assurance that it is the Lord who builds his Church and the gates of hell will not prevail against that Church. For a Church that is no longer convinced of truth needs to rediscover Jesus as the Truth, and should be willing, if need be, to die for that truth, which is Jesus. If we do not have the courage to speak the truth in love and witness to our faith we shall be like the Church in the early days of Islam which succumbed and was eradicated.

The most devout and sincere Muslims include those who are most active in seeking political power. Concern for the welfare of Muslims should not diminish our concern for the countries in which we live. Where the Judaeo-Christian ethic is the basis of society, this should not be abandoned or diluted, but rather affirmed. The revival of political Islam in the last few decades means that a re-evaluation of the present crisis in Christian-Muslim relations is necessary. It is not wise to continue harking back to the memory of the "good old days" that occurred under colonialism and before the rise of radical Islam, which on closer inspection may not have been so harmonious anyway.

Although superficially similar, Islam and Christianity are very far from being sibling religions. Not only does Islam specifically deny a series of key theological beliefs and creedal statements of Christianity, but also the whole basis of the faith is different. Christianity is based

on the premise that God is love. "Only from the pers-
pective of God's all-surpassing love revealed in Christ
can man finally acknowledge that love is the meaning of
reality (cf. John 3:16; Romans 5:6-11)."[82] Duty and works
are in vain. Islam is based on the premise that God is
power. Again duty and works are in vain but for a different
and terrifying reason – God acts on whim and cannot be
depended on.

If "love is the meaning of reality" for Christians, then
power is the meaning of reality for Muslims. Power and
its accompanying prestige must be gained at all costs.
There is no place in Islam for a suffering God, and human
vulnerability is likewise spurned. But the glory of Christianity is the vulnerability and human suffering borne out
of our understanding of the suffering of God in Christ
Jesus. To the Muslim mind this is an appalling thought.

In the Gospel we encounter God in Christ who reco-
nciles the world to himself. The suffering Christ is none
other than the redeemer of the world. To share him
means to witness to his redemptive and vicarious death,
even to our Muslim friends and neighbours. We are called
to rediscover what Paul means in sharing the whole
counsel of God with tears and trembling. The love of
Christ must renew and move the Church afresh to see
him more clearly, love him more dearly, follow him more
nearly and confess him more boldly in our day and age.
This is the road to recover a new confidence in the
Gospel.

Christian spirituality is founded on a suffering God
who sent his only Son to earth, taking the form of a
servant and sacrificing himself for humankind. The vulnerability and powerlessness that characterise the Christian

---

82   John M. McDermott *The Bible on Human Suffering* (Slough: St Paul Publications, 1990)
      p.141

faith must also define the relationship of Christians to Muslims. There can be no hate, bigotry or fear. The Christian modelled after his or her Master will seek the salvation of Muslims, in the words of Raymond Lull, "by love, by tears and by self-giving". In conclusion, as we explore relations between Muslims and Christians it is vital that we seek scholarly accuracy, that our hearts are filled with compassionate concern for Muslims as human beings, and that we remain utterly faithful to Christ and to his revelation.

APPENDIX: TEN CHRISTIAN APPROACHES TO ISLAM

In approaching Muslims, there are at least ten methods which are currently used in the West. This is not an exhaustive list, and there are no doubt other approaches as well. The various approaches are not necessarily to be treated in isolation from each other. Furthermore, not all of the ten listed below are compatible with the traditional understanding of the Bible's teaching.

1. *Evangelistic.* Christians who are primarily motivated by the conviction that Muslims need salvation through Jesus Christ will often seek common ground with Islam as a basis from which to share the Gospel message with the aim of conversion. Their aim is to focus on similarities between Islam and Christianity rather than differences. Further aspects of evangelism include intercessory prayer for Muslims, friendship evangelism, literature and various forms of contextualised ministry as well as signs and wonders.

2. *Caring and serving.* This approach is one of love and concern for the personal needs of individual Muslim friends and neighbours. It may involve assistance with material or physical needs, friendship for the lonely and isolated, condolences and celebrations for family events as appropriate, etc. In order for this to be biblical *diakonia* it must not be done in isolation but must include a spiritual and evangelistic dimension.

3. *Apologetic*. This is the approach of defending and explaining clearly the Christian faith to Muslim listeners. This involves the defence of doctrines of the Christian faith which Muslims attack, for example, the deity and death of Christ, the reliability of the Bible, as well as explaining aspects of the Christian faith which are misunderstood in Islam, for example, the Sonship of Christ and the Trinity. (1 Peter 3:15; 2 Timothy 2:15)

4. *Didactic*. Church leaders who teach their members about Islam must emphasise the differences between Islam and Christianity. In this way they will equip Christians to be able to resist the approaches of Muslims seeking to convert them to Islam, and give them a balanced understanding of the whole of Islamic doctrine and practice. This is necessary because what is presented in the secular media and by Muslims themselves on the nature of Islam is often only partial and sometimes even misleading. Such teaching will address the confusion which currently exists concerning the inter-relationship of Islam and Christianity and will especially address the popular concept of Islam and Christianity sharing the same beliefs and moral values in contradistinction to the secular world. This approach contrasts with the "common ground" approach involved in evangelism.

5. *Eschatological*. Some Christians view Islam as playing an important part in the End Times. For example, some have equated Islam with the antichrist of John's epistles. It is worth noting that the second coming of Jesus figures highly in Islamic eschatology together with the beast, the antichrist and Armageddon (see page 17). Although Islam is clear about its own position in the End Times, it is difficult for Christians to be so sure because it is not clearly delineated in the Bible.

6. *Motivated by justice*. These Christians are concerned with the rights of Christian and other non-Muslim minorities under Islam, where they are denied full human rights and religious liberty (see *dhimmi* status pages 66-68 and the Islamic law of apostasy pages 68-69,91-93). They seek to address issues of injustice, discrimination, violence and other abuses of human rights, and in order to accomplish this have to critique and criticise the relevant parts of Islam.

7. *Reconciliatory*. Some Christians seek to cooperate with Muslims on social issues of mutual concern. Reconciliation increasingly involves bringing Muslims and Christians together whether it is to campaign to change abortion laws or to bring warring factions together for peace talks. This is a non-biblical use of the word "reconciliation" (see page 88) and while it may be necessary for religions to be involved in finding solutions for global problems, it is highly questionable whether "reconciliation" is the best term to describe the process. Perhaps a better word would be "cooperation".

8. *Societal*. Islam, alone among world faiths, has very clear-cut aims for reorganising society to conform to its teaching. Because of this, Muslim minorities are impacting their host societies in the West in a way which no other faith is doing. Christians with a concern for their society and who recognise that Islam is more than just personal belief are active in seeking to alert decision-makers at national and local level to the implications of changes which are being made to accommodate the Muslim community in such areas as law, finance and education. This increasingly involves both social and political action.

9. *Dialogical*. This stance is most common amongst Western Christians whose main concern is for good community relations within their own countries. In interfaith discussions they will highlight as much that is positive in Islam as they can and eschew any discussion of subjects where a difference of opinion could arise. The subject of "dialogue" (and the various meanings given to that term) is dealt with in more depth on pages 80-83. Western governments are increasingly using "dialogue" as a method for tackling the ideological war between Islam and the West, and are seeking to utilise Church leaders in this pursuit. In other words, Western governments are using the Church as a way of engaging the Muslim world in order to neutralise theologies of violence and to establish cooperative relationships and ventures. The danger is that this practice will reinforce amongst Muslims their erroneous belief that all Western nations are ideologically Christian, and hence justify the persecution of Christian minorities in Muslim countries by radical Islamist groups. This politicisation of the Church for Western political interests is reminiscent of the colonial period and is likely to have dire consequences for the Church in the Muslim world today. It could also diminish the effectiveness of the Western Church with regard to her witness to Muslim minorities in the West.

10. *Pluralistic*. Many Christians regard Islam as theologically compatible with Christianity and therefore a valid alternative faith. Their approach to Muslims is like their approach to Christians, viewing both as "people of faith" ranged together against unbelievers. This book has sought to show that the two faiths are in fact mutually exclusive.

Although this book has been concerned with the situation in the West where Muslims are a minority, it is interesting to note that Christians who are living as minorities in Muslim-majority contexts would have a somewhat different list of possible approaches. For them the pressing issue would be how they can live in a Muslim-majority society where all too often they do not have full civic rights and religious liberty. Their concerns would be to maintain the distinctiveness of Christianity whilst simultaneously working for good relations with Muslims and, if allowed, for equal rights. They would also be concerned to be able to witness to their faith in situations of discrimination and persecution.

GLOSSARY OF ARABIC TERMS

Note: Arabic may be transliterated into English in a variety of ways, so the same Arabic word may be seen with alternative spellings indicating a similar sound e.g. *hudud* and *hudood*, *Qur'an* and *Koran*.

Allah – God. Used by all Muslims and by Arabic-speaking Christians, but with different understandings of the nature and character of God

auliya' – friends, protectors, helpers

dajjal – antichrist

Dar al-harb – literally "House of War". Classical Islam's term for territory not under Islamic rule

Dar al-Islam – literally "House of Islam" i.e. territory under Islamic rule

da'wa – call or invitation to Islam i.e. Muslim mission

dhikr - literally "remembrance". Meditative repetition of a short phrase, word or part of a word with the aim of achieving a trance-like state of union with Allah

dhimmi – literally "protected people". Christians, Jews and Sabeans under a Muslim government. They were permitted to live and keep their own faith in return for payment of *jiyza* and adherence to various demeaning regulations

fatiha – the first *sura* of the Qur'an, which has a central place in Islam, somewhat like that of the Lord's Prayer in Christianity

fatwa – an authoritative statement on a point of Islamic law

hadd (plural *hudud*) – punishments laid down in the Qur'an or *hadith* for certain specific crimes, and therefore mandatory under Islamic law e.g. amputation for theft, stoning for adultery

halal – permitted by Islamic law (often used of food)

hadith – traditions recording what Muhammad and his earliest followers said and did. Some traditions are considered more authentic and reliable than others

haram – forbidden by Islamic law

hajj – pilgrimage to Mecca

hudud – see *hadd*

irtidad – apostasy, leaving the Islamic faith

ijtihad – literally "effort" or "exertion". A legal procedure used to derive *shari'a* rules for situations which the Qur'an and *hadith* do not cover directly or by direct analogy

Islam – literally "submission" i.e. submission to the will
of Allah

Jibrail – Gabriel (the angel)

jihad – literally "striving". The term has a variety of
interpretations including (1) spiritual struggle for moral
purity (2) trying to correct wrong and support right by
voice and actions (3) military war against non-Muslims
with the aim of spreading Islam

jinn – a spirit, created by Allah. There are some good
jinn but many are evil

jizya – poll tax payable by *dhimmi* as a sign of their
subjugation to Muslims

julus – Sufi religious procession

ka'ba – cube shaped shrine at Mecca

kafir (plural *kafirun* or *kuffar*) – infidel i.e. non-Muslim.
This is a term of gross insult

kalima – another term for *shahada*

Kharijis – literally "seceders"; a puritanical sect of Islam
with a highly developed doctrine of sin. Sinners were
considered apostates. The sect began in 657 as a result
of disputes over the succession to the caliphate, and
continued to rebel against the caliphate for two
centuries. They survive today in a more moderate
variant, the Ibadis. (Arabic sing. *khariji*, Arabic pl.
khawarij)

kuffar – see *kafir*

kufr – unbelief (includes apostasy, blasphemy, heresy)

madrassa – Islamic religious school

Mahdi – the awaited End-Time deliverer

masjid – mosque

muezzin – one who makes the ritual call to prayer from the minaret or door of a mosque, in order to summon Muslims to pray

Qur'an – the holy book of Islam, comprising a series of "revelations" which Muhammad believed Allah gave him over the period 610 to 632

rasul – apostle, prophet, messenger

Ruh ul'Amin – literally "the Holy Spirit", used in Islam to mean the angel Gabriel

qunoot – special prayer for times of trouble

salam – peace. A common greeting among Muslims is *as-salamu 'alaikum* meaning "the peace be on you"

salat – ritual prayer, which Muslims must perform five times a day

sawm – fasting

shahada – the Islamic creed: "There is no god but God,

and Muhammad is the apostle of God." Also used of the act of reciting the creed in Arabic.

shari'a – literally "the way". Islamic law

Shi'a – the second largest branch of Islam, which broke away from the main body in 657

Sufi – a follower of Islamic mysticism

Sunni – the largest branch of Islam, comprising over 80% of Muslims today. Shi'as and Kharijis broke away from this main body

sura – chapter of the Qur'an

taqiyya – permitted deceit or dissimulation, applicable only in certain situations

tawhid – oneness; the fundamental doctrine of Islam declaring the absolute unity and indivisibility of God

umma – the whole body of Muslims worldwide

Wahhabi – member of a puritanical reform movement of Sunni Islam founded in the eighteenth century AD. Wahhabis are dominant in Saudi Arabia

zakat – the obligatory alms due from every Muslim

zikr – see *dhikr*

INDEX OF BIBLE REFERENCES

INDEX OF QUR'AN REFERENCES

Note: Verse numbers vary slightly between different translations of the Qur'an, so it may be necessary to search in the verses just preceding or just following the verse numbers given here to find the relevant text in any given translation.

INDEX OF *HADITH* REFERENCES

INDEX